The History
of Animals:
A Philosophy

ALSO AVAILABLE FROM BLOOMSBURY

The Animal Catalyst, edited by Patricia MacCormack
Eco-Aesthetics, Malcolm Miles
Ecosophical Aesthetics, edited by Colin Gardiner and
Patricia MacCormack
Environmental Ethics, Marion Hourdequin
General Ecology, edited by Erich Horl with James Burton
Posthuman Glossary, edited by Rosi Braidotti and Maria Hlavajova

The History of Animals: A Philosophy

Oxana Timofeeva

Introduction by Slavoj Žižek

BLOOMSBURY ACADEMIC

LONDON • NEW YORK • OXFORD • NEW DELHI • SYDNEY

BLOOMSBURY ACADEMIC
Bloomsbury Publishing Plc
50 Bedford Square, London, WC1B 3DP, UK
1385 Broadway, New York, NY 10018, USA
29 Earlsfort Terrace, Dublin 2, Ireland

BLOOMSBURY, BLOOMSBURY ACADEMIC and the Diana logo are
trademarks of Bloomsbury Publishing Plc

First published in Great Britain 2018
Reprinted 2018 (twice), 2019, 2022, 2023

Cover design by Irene Martinez Costa
Cover illustration © Luisa Lorenza Corna

A catalogue record for this book is available from the British Library.

A catalog record for this book is available from the Library of Congress.

ISBN: HB: 978-1-3500-1200-4
       PB: 978-1-3500-1201-1
       ePDF: 978-1-3500-1199-1
       eBook: 978-1-3500-1202-8

Typeset by Integra Software Services Pvt. Ltd.
Printed and bound in Great Britain

To find out more about our authors and books visit www.bloomsbury.com
and sign up for our newsletters.

Oh horse, you mustn't, oh horse, listen, horse:
  don't think you are worse than they are!
We are all of us horses, to some extent! Horse?

Vladimir Mayakovsky

Contents

Acknowledgements

This book was written, and the first, rather 'draft', version of it published in 2012 as a result of my work at the Jan van Eyck Academy in Maastricht, where I was a researcher in 2010–2011. These were two happiest years of my life, and I am thankful to all those who shared them with me. I would like to thank Mike Lewis, whose help in preparing this new edition was enormous, Slavoj Žižek for being the very first reader of the very first draft, Katja Diefenbach for pushing this project forward, Mladen Dolar for endlessly inspiring me, and Luisa Lorenza Corna for the wonderful cover. My special thanks are to my friends and colleagues from various fields, who read my work, commented on it, engaged with it or just shared with me their ideas, which are priceless – to Aaron Schuster, Benjamin Noys, Lorenzo Chiesa, Jamila Mascat, Katja Kolšek, Gregor Moder, Agon Hamza, Dominique Hurth, Dominiek Hoens, Nathaniel Boyd, Rasmus Ugilt, Sami Khatib, Steven Cuzner, Nina Power, Nikolay Poselyagin, Mikhail Iampolski and the entire 'Chto Delat' group; I am grateful to Valery Podoroga, Irina Prокhorova, Susanne

Frank and Artemy Magun for their support, and to Bloomsbury Publishing for this collaboration; I would like to thank my mom Galina Timofeeva, who taught me everything, my husband Andrey Zmeul, my sister Elena Goncharova, and other family members and relatives for their love; and, finally, I thank all animals living and dead and those who are not included in this list.

Preface

*I*n December 2015 I visited Ramallah, West Bank, where I attended a conference on Walter Benjamin.[1] These occupied territories are now surrounded by the wall. In order to get there, one needs to pass through a checkpoint. When I was leaving, I went through Kalandia checkpoint. Upon crossing the gates, I looked back: the land I've just visited stayed there behind that ugly, grey wall; I saw some roofs and mosque minarets. The wall was about three meters long, with a barbwire on the top. Suddenly, a bird flew above the wall – from what we call Israel to what we call Palestine. This book was completed three years earlier. When I was writing its concluding paragraph, the image of an animal crossing the borders and ignoring the gates was abstract; I did not have in mind any particular 'example' of such animal. It could have been some other beast, crossing some other gate, but nothing less than history itself brought me to that place at that moment of time and made me see this audacious bird.

The History of Animals is the title taken from Aristotle. I borrowed it on purpose – I wanted to provide this combination of two words with a new sense and to give credit for what must be comprehended as historical animality. My major premise is that, gainsaying the fact that animals have traditionally been consigned to non-historical nature, they do *have a history*. They have their own historical materiality, at the very least as a labour force. However, the logic of their history does not conform, in my view, to the optimism of the humanistic discourse of the progressive liberation and emancipation of animals that would finally secure their rights. Quite the contrary, it seems rather that from ancient totemism, inspired by the greatness of animal ancestors, through the sequence of exclusions and inclusions, to the present tragedy and farce that combine slaughterhouses, pet shops and global safaris, animals have had a bad 'career'. Historically, they have failed.

In his wonderful essay *Why Look at Animals?* John Berger claims that 'in the last two centuries, animals have gradually disappeared' (Berger 2009: 21). According to Berger, the disappearance of animals is the process simultaneous with the appearance of zoos: 'Public zoos came into existence at the beginning of the period which was to see the disappearance of animals from daily life' (30). What is the period at stake? We are not talking about a mere abstract chronology; nothing but capitalist modernity is concerned: 'The historic loss, to which zoos are the monument, is now irredeemable for the culture of capitalism' (37). More and more animals depart, one by one, leaving humanity with their own representations, with pets and toys. To these striking observations, Akira Mizuta Lippit adds that in fact they 'never *entirely* vanish', but rather continue to exist 'in a state of *perpetual vanishing*'. Their existence become *spectral*, or, 'In supernatural terms, modernity finds animals lingering in the world *undead*' (Lippit 2000: 1). While disappearing from our everyday life, the spectres of animals reappear in arts, theory and visual culture. In philosophy, too, they become not only ghosts but welcome guests: I am not original in my desire to follow their scent here. What I propose is to read the history of philosophy as the history of animals. This is my essay's general ambition, if I might call it so.

What does philosophy have to say about the animal? It appears that the common attitude can be inscribed into a traditional pattern of ascending hierarchy. Already in Aristotle the idea may be found that animals are 'better' than plants, that humans are 'better' than animals, that men are 'better' than women, free citizens 'better' than slaves and so on. Not because whatever is inferior is 'bad', but because whoever is superior knows better what is 'good'. Even those who clearly 'side with' animality, and fight for animal rights and animal liberation with the ultimate aim of achieving an equal representation of the animal species in this still all-too-human world, cannot do away with the idea of the domination (now widely criticized) of mankind over non-human nature, as if the latter really needed our help, respect, support, recognition.

Animals in fact do not really care about human's care for them: we sacrifice them, transport them to the slaughterhouse, eat them, exploit them, train them, involve them in art processes and give them rights and documents – but they remain indifferent. (This may not apply to pets and other domesticated animals, whose individual survival directly depends on humans, which makes them pretend a limited interest in response to man's desperate attempts to attract their attention.)

The moral attitude of humans towards animals can easily be brought back to its affective root, to the level of desire, which underlies any ethical concern or pragmatic preoccupation. Would it not be fair to say that the flip side of ascending hierarchy is a descending degree of jealousy and envy? Sometimes philosophers – being perhaps the most arrogant of humans – are really jealous of the animal's taking pleasure in things, which the animals, so they think, nevertheless cannot fully experience as they are not fully conscious of their own enjoyment. As Bataille has it,

> Man, despite appearances, must know that when he talks about human dignity in the presence of animals, he lies like a dog. For in the presence of illegal and essentially free beings (the only real outlaws) the stupid feeling of practical superiority gives way to a most uneasy envy. (Bataille 1986: 22–23)

The representation of animality is one of the principal issues at stake in the currently expanding theoretical debates on animals. Long after the Cartesian verdict, the philosophy of animality is turning to the question of how to think animal existence – which, supposedly, does not think itself. A consensus has recently been reached that we cannot deal with animality as such, but only with the human construction of animality. In addition, it is believed that in a sense 'the animal does not exist', as if it were in the end nothing besides its own representation. The animal cannot but be represented, which means that it is either a representation or a representative. A representation gives us an external idea of what an animal is as an object (such as those we find in art, popular science or mass culture). An animal as representative comprises a figuration of its interest as a subject (in the animal rights movement, for instance, as well as in animal studies that critically relate themselves to the human sciences).

However, in what now seems a bygone cultural tradition, animals played a much more active role, serving as representatives of something human or divine, as in totemism or antiquity. For example, Incitatus, Caligula's favourite horse, became not only a citizen of Rome but a member of the Roman senate as well. This is a truly ridiculous manifestation of the embodiment of representative power. In classical narratives, animals traditionally represent human qualities and weaknesses. To take some more recent examples, in psychoanalysis animals might represent human agents associated with law and order, like the wolf that represents the father in Freud's famous case of the 'Wolf Man'. In turn, this inevitable representational frame makes the idea of a real animal possible, which rather than being represented or representing something already given instead opens the immediate givenness of the 'real' of the human being itself, albeit retrospectively. The ambiguity of the animal, which is a representation par excellence, and yet at the same time also unrepresentable, provokes a particular tension between ontology, politics and psychoanalysis, and it is interesting to track the ways in which animal is produced in the very unstable field of the 'human'.

Philosophers have always made the distinction between human beings and animals, giving rational thought, language or the awareness of death as criteria. There are two types of classical philosophical discourse that focus on the animal: the discourse of *exclusion* begins from the ethical and ontological predominance of the 'human', whereas the discourse of *inclusion* insists on the affinity of all levels of being. But these two discourses are related and their function is the same: to establish or conserve a certain *order of things*. As Bataille pointed out, the basis of this rational order is the transcendence of the 'human', which requires the sacrifice of irreducible 'animal' nature. The cosmic order, the state order, the world order and, finally, the symbolic order – they will all count in this alternative history, which could aim to radicalize animality if it were not already radical enough.

Regarding madness, Foucault says that animality is its internal truth, a truth which reveals the limits of the 'human' (Foucault 1965). Animality is like an unthinking, unthinkable mirror-twin of subjectivity. According to Lacan, looking into the mirror, the human being appropriates its own image as 'human' in a form originally exterior to itself (Lacan 1977: 1–7). But what if it is the animal that exists outside of the mirror, where the human being has to recognize itself and at the same time cannot do so. Re-reading Lacan, Derrida specifies that the real enigma is to be found not in the human being gazing at its own mirror reflection, but rather in the animal that stares back at the human (Derrida 2003).

The play of inside and outside, inclusion and exclusion, is a kind of device that Agamben calls an 'anthropological machine'; it establishes a borderline between the self and the 'animal' other. Again, lacanian metaphor can be applied to this optical device:

the human being recognizes itself in the animal as it does in the mirror. This is a kind of mirror stage, which is to say the moment when human starts to acquire his humanity. Recognizing himself in the animal, he begins to distinguish himself from it:

> *Homo sapiens*, then, is neither a clearly defined species nor a substance; it is, rather, a machine or device for producing the recognition of the human. ... It is an optical machine constructed from a series of mirrors in which man, looking at himself, sees his own image always already deformed in the features of an ape. *Homo* is a constitutively 'anthropomorphous' animal ..., who must recognize himself in a non-man in order to be human. (Agamben 2004: 26)

But this mirror-machine operates in two directions. Recognition is always accompanied by misrecognition. Man recognizes himself in the animal until the common anthropomorphic world breaks up into two parts and the mirror stands between him and his other, and a gap or lacuna necessarily opens up. For Agamben, this is not only a metaphysical but also a political operation:

> The machine of earlier times works in an exactly symmetrical way. If, in the machine of the moderns, the outside is produced through the exclusion of an inside and the inhuman produced by animalizing the human, here the inside is obtained through the inclusion of an outside, and the non-man is produced by the humanization of an animal: the man-ape, the *enfant sauvage* or *Homo ferus*, but also and above all the slave, the barbarian, and the foreigner, as figures of an animal in human

form. ...And faced with this extreme figure of the human and the inhuman it is not so much a matter of asking which of the two machines (or of the two variants of the same machine) is better or more effective – or, rather, less lethal and bloody – as it is of understanding how they work so that we might, eventually, be able to stop them. (2004: 37–38)

Unlike Agamben, I do not pretend to stop the anthropological machine, to sabotage the machine of metaphysics, which supposedly devours the living energy of the animal that is hidden inside it, like a horsepower at the heart of the mechanism. I just want to take a certain position from which it will be possible to investigate whether the very same machine can work differently.

While doing research on certain figures that are obviously repressed in the Western philosophical tradition, especially animals and animality, one encounters a very specific style or strategy adopted by contemporary critics: to accuse thinkers of the past of treating animals badly. This particular form of philosophical projection is, of course, a necessary part of the Oedipal scenario of the relationship with the fathers of philosophy, and such a topic as animality provides an immense amount of leeway for that. No doubt, philosophers of the past, grounded in metaphysics, theology, rationalism or humanism, used to take anthropocentric, speciesist, sexist, racist or Eurocentric approaches, and every attempt at a critical deconstruction of their thought reaches a unanimous verdict.

It is understandable that, in the posthumanist tradition, thinkers such as Descartes or Hegel, but also Heidegger and

Levinas, are widely categorized as 'enemies', but sometimes even Deleuze, who was among the first to make a serious attempt to get rid of anthropocentrism by proclaiming the becoming-animal as a true philosophical attitude, or Derrida, this, shall we say, animal philosopher *par excellence*, who dedicated his last works to animality (Derrida 2008, 2009–2011), who criticizes not only Heidegger but also Lacan for his anthropo-phallo-logo-centrism and brings up the question of animals theoretically within the programme of the deconstruction of the subject, can come under suspicion (de Fontenay 1998; Wood 1999). As if there was a kind of competition in passing judgement on previous philosophers for their maltreatment of animals. We shall, as Lenin says, go another way. I would prefer to avoid the rhetoric of judgement and not participate in the trial, not because I want to justify philosophers before an animal kingdom, but because I insist on the principal ambiguity of every single philosopher.

This book is not a philosophical bestiary: I do not touch upon the question of animal symbolism, but rather focus on a 'naïve', literal, 'direct' or symptomatic reading of the metaphysical tradition, respecting the rules of its games even though these rules are always already outdated, without pretending to unveil a certain 'reality' behind these games. The narrative structure that is at stake here works without being necessarily exposed in a framework of a kind of 'critical realism' that refers to a current state of affairs. In my *History of Animals*, humans, things, souls, cosmos, alienation, communism and so on are all characters, playing their part in a metaphysical scenario, written by no one.

Introduction by
Slavoj Žižek

In his book *Structure, Logic, Alienation*, François Balmès notes
that the ongoing progress of biogenetics

> disrupts the conditions of human reproduction and radically
> disconnects it from the encounter of the two sexes, thus
> opening the possibility of generalised eugenics, of the
> fabrication of clones, monsters, or hybrids, which shatters
> the limits of a species. The limits of the biological real are
> effectively displaced, and the most secure constraints of
> what is symbolised, life, death, filiation, bodily identity, the
> difference of the sexes, are rendered friable. Cloning allows
> us in principle to get rid of a partner, and thereby of the other
> sex, or of alterity as such: one perpetuates oneself without
> alteration. There is a historical mutation in this which is
> at least as radical as the death of the human species made
> possible by nuclear fission. (Balmès 2011: 16)

This process which will change the very definition of human being forms the historical background of the questions raised by Oxana Timofeeva in this wonderful book: it is precisely today, when humanity seems on the verge of leaving its animality behind, that the question of the animal returns with a vengeance. No wonder the last part of this book is dedicated to Andrei Platonov – together with Beckett and Kafka, one of the three absolute writers of the twentieth century – whose work focuses on the aspects of technological gadgets replacing sex as well as our affinity with animals and our solidarity with them.

In late 1925, Platonov wrote a short essay called 'Anti-Sexus'.[1] He presents himself as the translator of a propaganda brochure of a large Western company that wants to make headway in the Soviet market. After giving the translator's introduction, the company's head describes the product, and what then follow are the short quotes of well-known public figures (from Mussolini to Gandhi, from Henry Ford to Charles Chaplin, from J.M. Keynes to Marshall Hindenburg) about the product, a mass-produced masturbatory machine that allows the user to reach fast and intense orgasm. In this way, humanity can be relieved of the intricacies of sexual love. Sexual need loses its uncontrollable character; it no longer involves the time- and energy-consuming process of seduction and becomes available to everyone in a simple and planned way, thus promising a new era of inner peace. Although 'Anti-Sexus' is obviously a satirical piece, things get complicated the moment we try to determine the precise objective of satire. It is usually taken that Chaplin's comment – the only negative one: the product will deprive us of the intense and deeply spiritual intersubjective contact which characterizes genuine sexual love – stands for the position of Platonov himself, but does it? Is the profound distrust of sexual love not the main feature of Platonov's work throughout the 1920s?

Platonov's two great novels from the late 1920s (*Chevengur* and, especially, *The Foundation Pit*) are usually interpreted as a critical depiction of the Stalinist utopia and its disastrous consequences. However, the utopia Platonov portrays in these two works is not that of Stalinist Communism, but the Gnostic-materialist utopia, against which 'mature' Stalinism reacted in the early 1930s. Dualist-Gnostic motifs prevail in this utopia: sexuality and the entire bodily domain of generation or corruption are perceived as a hated prison to be overcome by the scientific construction of a new ethereal and desexualized immortal body. (This is why Zamyatin's dystopia *We* is also not a critical portrayal of the totalitarian potential of Stalinism, but the extrapolation of the Gnostic-utopian tendency of the revolutionary 1920s, against which, precisely, Stalinism reacted. In this sense, Althusser was right and not involved in cheap paradoxes when he insisted that Stalinism was a form of humanism: its 'cultural counter-revolution' was a humanist reaction against the 'extremist' Gnostic-utopian post-humanist 1920s.) We should also bear in mind that from the outset Lenin opposed this Gnostic-utopian orientation (which attracted, among others, Trotsky and Gorky) with its dream of a shortcut to the new Proletarian Culture or the New Man. Nonetheless, one should perceive this Gnostic utopianism as a kind of 'symptom' of Leninism, as the manifestation of what made the revolution fail, as the seed of its later 'obscure disaster'. That is to say, the question to be raised here is, Is the utopian universe depicted by Platonov the extrapolation of the immanent logic of the Communist revolution or the extrapolation of the logic that underlies the activity of those who precisely fail to follow the script of a 'normal' Communist revolution and engage in a millenarist shortcut that is destined to end in dismal failure? How does the idea of a Communist revolution stand in regard to the millenarist idea of the instant actualization of the utopia? Furthermore, can these two options be clearly distinguished? Was there ever a 'proper' and 'ripe' Communist revolution? And if not, what does this mean for the very concept of the Communist revolution?

Platonov was in a constant dialogue with this pre-Stalinist utopian core, which is why his final 'intimate' ambiguous love/ hate engagement with the Soviet reality related to the renewed utopianism of the first five-year plan; after that, with the rise of High Stalinism and its cultural counter-revolution, the coordinates of the dialogue changed. In so far as High Stalinism was anti-utopian, Platonov's turn towards a more 'conformist' Socialist-Realist writing in the 1930s cannot be dismissed as a mere external accommodation due to much stronger censorship and oppression: it was rather an immanent easing of tensions, up to a point even a sign of sincere proximity. The High and late Stalinism had other immanent critics (Grossman, Shalamov, Solzhenytsin, etc.) who were in 'intimate' dialogue with it, sharing its underlying premises.

This is why Platonov remains an ambiguous embarrassment for later dissidents. The key text of his 'Socialist Realist' period is the short novel *The Soul* (1935), and although the typically

Platonov's utopian group is still here – the 'nation', a desert community of marginal people who have lost the will to live – the coordinates have completely changed. The hero is now a Stalinist educator, schooled in Moscow; he returns to the desert to introduce the 'nation' to scientific and cultural progress and thus restore their will to live. (Platonov, of course, remains faithful to his ambiguity: at the end of the novel, the hero has to accept that he cannot teach others anything.) This shift is signalled by the radically altered role of sexuality: for the Platonov of the 1920s, sexuality was the anti-utopian 'dirty' power of inertia, while here, it is rehabilitated as the privileged path to spiritual maturity – although he fails as an educator, the hero finds spiritual solace in sexual love, such that it is as if the 'nation' is almost reduced to the background of the creation of a sexual couple.

This brings us back to the 'Anti-Sexus': the importance of this essay resides in paradoxically bringing together three orientations which are independent of each other and sometimes even antagonistic, namely the Gnostic equation of sex with the Fall (the Russian sect of Skopcy whose male members voluntarily castrated themselves deeply impressed Platonov), the biotechnological prospect of total regulation or even abolition of sex and capitalist consumerism. Modern biotechnology provides a new way of realizing the old Gnostic dream of getting rid of sex – however, the gadget which does it comes from capitalism and presents itself as the ultimate commodity. Therein resides the subterranean tension of Platonov's essay: the new masturbatory gadget brings together these three (or even four) elements: Gnostic spiritualism, the reign of modern science, Soviet total regulation of life and the capitalist universe of profit-making commodities. Multiple relations are possible here, such as the tech-Gnostic vision of combining the first two (a technologically regulated spiritual withdrawal of humans), the capitalist commodification of our innermost experience (orgasm), a spiritualized Communism which tends towards a 'post-human' overcoming of sexuality and so on. What makes the essay so rich, in spite of its narrative simplicity, is the lack of a general 'cognitive mapping': Where does the masturbatory machine belong within the space of these four coordinates? It is interesting to note that a similar celebration of desexualized vitality abounds in Stalinism. Although the Stalinist total mobilization during the first five-year plan tended to fight sexuality as the last domain of bourgeois resistance, this did not prevent it from trying to recuperate sexual energy in order to reinvigorate the vitality of the struggle for socialism – in the early 1930s, a variety of 'tonics' were widely advertised in the Soviet media, with names like 'Spermin-pharmakon', 'Spermol' and 'Sekar fluid – Extractum testiculorum' (Platonov 2009: 206).

With today's hindsight, the gadget imagined by Platonov neatly fits into the ongoing shift in the predominant libidinal economy, in the course of which the relationship to the Other is gradually replaced by the captivation of individuals by what late Lacan baptised with the neologism '*les lathouses*', consumerist object-gadgets which attract the libido with their promise of excessive pleasure, but effectively reproduce only the lack itself. This is how psychoanalysis approaches the libidinal-subjective impact of new technological inventions: 'technology is a catalyser, it enlarges and enhances something which is already here' (Dolar 2008: 12) – in this case, a fantasmatic virtual fact, like that of a partial object. And, of course, this realization changes the entire constellation: once a fantasy is realized, once a fantasmatic object directly appears in reality, reality is no longer the same. And, effectively, one finds on today's market a gadget close to what Platonov imagined: the so-called 'Stamina Training Unit', a masturbatory device which resembles a torch (so that, when we carry it around, we are not embarrassed). You insert the erect penis into the opening at the top and move the thing up and down until satisfaction is achieved. The product is available in different colours, tightness and forms that imitate all three main openings for sexual penetration (mouth, vagina, anus). What one buys here is simply the partial object (erogenous zone) alone, deprived of the embarrassing additional burden of the entire person. The fantasy (of reducing the sexual partner to a partial object) is here directly realized, and this changes the entire libidinal economy of sexual relations.

How, then, can we break out of this depressing predicament? Oxana Timofeeva shows the way: the full acceptance of our animality, that is, an acceptance which does not mean 'the return to our animal roots', 'freely enjoying our instinctual sexuality', or anything similar. This acceptance goes through negativity, and freedom is an effect of a very paradoxical move, the necessity of which appears retrospectively as the very core of metaphysical philosophy and Christian culture, traditionally (and wrongly) opposed to our 'animal' nature and seemingly detached from it.

Slavoj Žižek

1

Oedipus the horse

In Book IX of *History of Animals*, Aristotle describes the characters of animals. The task of submitting the highly explosive orgy of natural life to a scientific order of representation requires a scrupulous attention to detail, even if the details seem insignificant or improbable. The sources of Aristotle's knowledge of animal's habits are not merely observations but also legends, rumours, anecdotes, stories told by people, eyewitness accounts. The prolific and extremely heterogeneous empirical material deserves special consideration. One should first establish and take into account all details and particularities, avoiding the temptation of simplification, reduction and hasty theoretical abstraction. Principles of classification are not so rigorous in this era, yet they do exist. Later on, one of the principles will be called anthropic.

Aristotle's fauna assume the dimensions of the human and are clearly human-like, not because of the supposed superiority of the human being, but rather because of his supposed capacity to understand himself. Human beings are not just part of this world; they are its universal model. Other creatures, the most weird and fantastic included, approximate this model to a greater or lesser extent and are endowed with certain human characteristics, such as friendliness or aggression, slyness or simple-mindedness, nobleness or baseness, audacity or timidity.

Animals are not only human-like – they also imitate humans in their own ways. It is not the other way around. A swallow that builds a nest imitates a human who builds a house:

> In general, with regard to their lives, one may observe many imitations of human life in the other animals, and more especially in the smaller than in the larger animals one may see the precision of their intelligence: for example, first, in the case of the birds, the swallow's nest-building. For in the mixing to straw into mud she keeps the same order. She interweaves mud with the stalks; and if she lucks mud she moistens herself and rolls her feathers into the dust. Further, she builds the nest just as men build, putting the stuff materials underneath first, and making it match herself in size. (Aristotle 1991: 253)

The word 'order' is important here. Respecting the order, Aristotle's swallow imitates human prudence. In a nutshell, one can argue that plants, animals and humans are doing the same work, albeit differently. Plants imitate animals, animals imitate humans and humans imitate the gods. They all respect some order in their lives. It is as if a bird and a human were maintaining some general order, as if they were sharing a rationally ordered world. In this world, to use Simondon's definition, there is a functional continuity that extends to all living things and provides them with a single principle – the principle of life:

Habit in animals is a kind of experience that imitates human prudence. Imitate here means that which is a functional analogue of the human prudence, but with different operatory modes … Thus, even if we admit it – and we have to admit it, that according to Aristotle reason is properly human and specifically characteristic of man, there exist continuities and functional equivalences within the various levels of organization between the different modes of living beings. (Simondon 2011: 49–50)

In *Two Lessons on Animal and Man*, Gilbert Simondon interprets a principle of life as an invariant in Aristotle's biological theory of functions. The presence of a *grand hypothèse* allows the theory to count as genuinely scientific (whereas the naturalistic conceptions of earlier authors are still hardly distinguishable from myth).[1] One should note, however, that this kind of science is deeply bound up with a general worldview and acquires its full meaning only within the whole of the metaphysical system, where even the modest decoration of a swallow's nest reflects the structure of the entire universe.

Mimesis makes it possible to organize an interchange between different levels of being. Animals, humans, plants – all are involved in a matter of great consequence, a maintenance of the cosmos. Consider the Aristotelian elephant greeting the king: 'The tamest and gentlest of all the wild animals is the elephant, for there are many things it both learns and understands: they are even taught to kneel before the king' (Aristotle 1991: 39). Each entity has its own way of maintaining this general hierarchical world order, in which above humans, there are also the divine heavenly bodies – the sun, stars and planets. As Aristotle writes in *Nichomachean Ethics*, 'It may be argued that man is superior to the other animals, but this makes no difference: since there exist other things far more divine in their nature then man, for instance, to mention the most visible, the things of which the celestial system is composed' (Aristotle 1926: 345). Aristotelian creatures do not make any particular effort to participate in this cause – they are just expected to do what they do naturally, at their specific place and in their specific manner. The order which all things maintain was not established by humans, but humans conceive themselves as the measure of it. Eventually, everyone in his or her own way already conforms to certain general laws and prohibitions, which seem all too human.

Chapter XLVII, which is comprised of two short stories, deserves further attention:

Camels do not cover their mothers, but refuse even if force is used. For on one occasion, when there was no stallion, the keeper put the mother's colt to her, after putting a wrap over her; when it fell away after the mating, by then he had completed the intercourse, but a little later he bit the camel-man to death.

It is said too that the king of the Scythians had a high-quality mare all of whose colts where good; the king, wishing to breed from the best out of the mother, brought it to her to mate; but it refused; but after she had been concealed under a wrap it mounted her in ignorance; and when the mare's face was uncovered after the mating, at sight of her the horse ran away and threw itself down the cliffs. (Aristotle 1991: 393)

This is truly a strange story. In fact, in contemporary ethology, it is assumed that some animals are really inclined to avoid 'incest'. Hence, the way of life that implies a relocation of younger generations to take up a new habitat reduces the possibility of an encounter with a parent as a sexual mate. Some scientists admit that this prohibition, which is cultural in humans, is natural in animals, and that it is reasonable and justified and in the objective interest of the species.

Theories of this kind are, however, contradicted by the fact that some polygamous animals enjoy a relative sexual freedom that does not do any damage to their offspring. What is more, certain ancient peoples already knew that inbreeding, or consanguineous mating, could generate positive results for the breed, and they used it widely in artificial selection. This is what they were pursuing in the Scythian king's stable, but 'it is said' that the horse offered a clear resistance to their attempts.

The scope of this text, however, is not to query a scientific truth that is related to the authenticity of sources or the objectivity and certainty of Aristotle's observations and speculations. We will not consider the problem of the proportion between cultural and natural factors in the origin of the prohibition of incest. We shall, instead, acknowledge that under the vault of the starry

Aristotelian heaven, both an inglorious poor man's camel and a thoroughbred king's horse behave in the only way they can – they are trying to observe a law.

The second story, in particular, refers to a well-known myth. The gesture of a groom concealing the mare under a wrap is a kind of parody of the blind fate that drives Oedipus into his mother Jocasta's arms. The scene of the animal galloping off to commit suicide immediately its mother's face is revealed is truly impressive: just picture the lonely, absurd figure of a horse fleeing in despair towards the abyss. What is the impulse of the 'animal soul' that urges it forward and down?

In Book VI of the *Nichomachean Ethics*, Aristotle writes thus: 'Even some of the lower animals are said to be prudent, namely those which display a capacity for forethought as regards their own life' (Aristotle 1926: 343). Yet, this kind of recognition, given to animals by chance, does not gainsay the basic fact that prudence 'is concerned with the affairs of men' (345). In Aristotle, of all animals only the human being is capable of producing independent reasonable judgement, that is, making reasonable choices and performing reasonable acts.

How is it possible, then, that a horse commits suicide? What is suicide, if not an act? One cannot call it prudent or reasonable: it is imprudent, unreasonable and reckless. And if we want to interpret this act with reference to the Aristotelian system, we should refer once again to the idea of mimesis, which grants continuity and succession to all living beings. An imprudent act on the part of an animal should then be regarded as a kind of imitation of an imprudent act on the part of man, performed in the same situation. If only the horse had hands, he would have blinded himself just as his human role model did. The Aristotelian horse behaves as if he were human. Indeed, his behaviour is all too human. He becomes human in the short vertiginous moment of his ultimate downfall.

It seems that the motif of the prohibition of incest is so widespread and pervasive in ancient Greek culture that it is projected onto animals. However, what is frightening is not incest *per se*, but the breach of a cosmic order that the act provokes. We should not forget that Oedipus the Horse, turned desperately imprudent, was born in a reasonably ordered world. The stability of the harmonious structure of this world is guaranteed by the participation of all its functional elements, even those which do so passively. A restricted failure imperils the entire system and threatens the principle of life as such.

By breaking down the traditional family hierarchy and the continuity from generation to generation, incestuous intercourse spells trouble for the entire community. Thus, in Sophocles' *Oedipus the King* it brings pestilence on the people of Thebes. One cannot but notice that a plague (crop failure, barrenness, mass mortality of humans and animals) may function as a symbolic substitute for 'degeneration', which is in some human cultures traditionally associated with endogamy. The horror of a woman giving birth to her husband conceived by her husband and birth to her children conceived by her own child amounts to a breakdown of some 'natural' or habitual course of life, a collapse of the regular line of reproduction, in a fatal short circuit.

At any point, the balance of the delicate cosmos can be disrupted, and this is the main danger posed by a breach in the order of things. However, a breach of the order, an individual's failure or a violence affecting the whole cannot be considered a crime. Rather, it is a fault or an error, because, generally speaking, it was performed out of ignorance or blindness. Nobody will do ill of his or her own volition, because the prudence of Aristotelian humans and human-like animals consists in pursuing what is good. Those who do ill simply do not understand what is good; they are not sufficiently reasonable, they are blinded by anger or some other passion or they are not acquainted with the law.

As far as the highest good and laws are concerned, one might suspect that they are known only to a select few, and these few are the ones leading the state. As is well known, the hierarchical state system, according to Aristotle, corresponds to human nature itself; wherein the soul rules the body and the mind rules the emotions. Animals, being less prudent, must be subordinate to humans, since through humans they join the highest good, just as woman does through her superior, man, and slaves do through free men. This is the famous Aristotelian justification for the system of slavery: slaves, he argues, are already slaves by nature, and even bodily they are closer to domestic animals, whose basic function is to do useful work, than to free men (Aristotle 1932: 19–21). One observes the law without knowing it if one obeys the people who *do* know. This is a painful situation, as Kafka suggests in one of his short stories, *The Problem of Our Laws*:

Our laws are not generally known; they are kept secret by the small group of nobles who rule us. We are convinced that these ancient laws are scrupulously administered; nevertheless it is an extremely painful thing to be ruled by laws that one does not know. (Kafka 1995: 437)

However, even those at the top of society, the rulers and the kings, the Kafkian nobles, can share this pain, as long as there is still another superior power that is higher in rank than they are, which is to say, an obscure god's will. It may seem absurd or unjust, but it has the force of law. Not knowing the law is no excuse. Thus, by observing the laws, which are beyond their understanding, both the king and the king's horse participate in the maintenance of the cosmos.

The Aristotelian human being is still a part of an immense family of living beings, all of which resemble him to a greater or lesser extent. He recognizes himself in animals and sees in their behaviour a kind of parody of his own gestures. He feels a deep affinity with them. This feeling obviously relates to totemism as well as the ancient Greek belief in metempsychosis, the fantastical circulation of *anima*, the living soul, among vegetable, animal and human bodies. Anima is still common; it has not yet been appropriated by anyone and therefore cannot yet be alienated.

One can imagine the unanimous ensemble of creatures involved in the common production of the strong unity of the ancient cosmos. The horse occupies a really important and honourable place in this ensemble. It is even represented on the flip side of Greek gold coins. In his essay 'The Academic

Horse', published in the first issue of the journal *Documents*, Georges Bataille reflects on the correlation between intellectual, social and bodily experiences and emphasizes the mathematical precision and nobility of the equine expression of harmony:

There is no reason to hesitate in pointing out that, as paradoxical as it might appear, the horse, situated by a curious coincidence at the origins of Athens, is one of the most accomplished expressions of the *idea*, just as much, for example, as Platonic philosophy or the architecture of the Acropolis. All representations of this animal during the classical age can be seen to extol, not without betraying a common arrogance, a profound kinship with Hellenic genius. Everything happened, in fact, as if the forms of the body as well as social forms or forms of thought tended towards a sort of ideal perfection from which all value proceeded; as if the progressive organization of these forms sought gradually to satisfy the immutable harmony and hierarchy that Greek philosophy tended characteristically to ascribe to *ideas*, external to concrete facts. And the fact remains that the people most submissive to the need to see noble and irrevocable ideas rule and lead the course of things, could easily translate its dread by portraying the body of a horse: the hideous or comical body of a spider or of a hippopotamus would not have corresponded to this elevation of spirit. (Ades and Baker 2006: 238)

Bataille compares the academic horse understood as the embodiment of the Greek *eidos* to the unrealistic, demented horses represented not on Greek but on Gallic coins. From around the fourth century BC, the Gauls began to mint their own coins, imitating Greek originals. But the image of the horse is significantly deformed here, and its deformations, according to Bataille, are not random. They are not merely the result of some technical lapse. Crazy barbarian horses are illustrations of a disordered life that is unfamiliar with the high ideals of harmony and perfection. This kind of life, full of excess, violence and danger, is bereft of these high ideals, like 'police regulations are to the pleasures of the criminal classes' (ibid.).

Bataille, whose sympathy is clearly with 'the criminal classes', describes the aesthetic degradation of the horse's image as a form of transgression and rebellion against the arrogance of a rationalist culture's idealism:

> The ignoble equidae monkeys and gorillas of the Gauls, animals with unspeakable morals and ugly beyond compare, but also grandiose apparitions, staggering wonders, thus represent a definitive response of the burlesque and frightful human night to the platitudes and arrogance of idealists. (ibid.)

The demented horses of the Gauls can be interpreted as a material trace of the process known as the 'regression to barbarism' or the 'return to the animal condition'. In the so-called civilized world, the smallest allusion to the possibility of such a process legitimates even the strongest forms of the maintenance of order and social hierarchy. All 'criminal classes' will be tamed by their own 'police regulations'.

Of course, the people at the top present chaos and barbarism as the ultimate (and undesirable) alternative to the *status quo*.

Were it not for wise police measures, the world would cease to be intelligible and anthropomorphic; the night would fall; and sweet, human-like Aristotelian animals would be displaced by maddened, barbaric monsters. Humans-horses would transform into ape-horses. Humans would themselves transform into animals. 'The equidae monkeys and gorillas', no longer possessing a human appearance, in contrast to Aristotelian swallows, would cease to care about keeping order, and, unlike the Aristotelian elephant, still less would they 'kneel before the king'.

Fear of entropy makes us fretful, and we ward it off with manifold rituals. It seems that the reproduction of the conditions of human life requires a permanent effort. Harmonious ancient forms serve to illustrate the fact that such efforts were not in vain. But it seems that the forces of chaos, such as floods, invasions, war, revolution, epidemics, volcanic explosions, which were heretofore just potential menaces, have taken over. Thus, the failure of leaving creatures to maintain these harmonious forms reveals the fragility of the cosmos.

The academic horse, represented on the Greek golden coin, is allied to the Oedipalized horse from Aristotle's book. However, the initially 'good' Aristotelian horse transgresses the bounds of order, goes mad and becomes an absurd self-murdering animal. There is no place for him in this glorious police world that obeys the laws he ignores. He is doomed to become an outcast, since he has come to know something that he should not have known, according to his rank. Perhaps it would have been better for him to put his trust in the human who knows better what is good for him, in his stableman, but he was doomed all the same.

Generally speaking, Aristotle's animals are all 'academic'. Even if they are not perfect, they are still human-like and therefore inoffensive. Aristotle places a great deal of trust in his animals, that they will be faithful to a kind of ontological unity, as a consequence of which the world can be rationally explained on the basis of general rules and laws. As I have already shown, this system presupposes a hierarchical order in which those who are less prudent (animals, slaves, women) are subjected to those who are more prudent.

Apparently the Aristotelian system does not presuppose external 'enemies', but all the more internal ones. It functions owing to the inclusion of all the elements, but it makes no provision for a situation in which, for example, the animal fails to imitate the human. In this case, the maintenance of the cosmos will become impossible. Can we then presuppose that if the mass of creatures that are unable to observe the rule reaches critical proportions, then the world, as we know it, will collapse?

This is rather the logic of another mode of 'protective thinking', by which I mean the discourse that immediately, positively identifies with a symbolic order based on a distrust of the alien – the logic of exclusion. Here, animal nature, unpredictable but also indifferent to the subtle artifices of intellectual and spiritual humanity that are so difficult to protect from accidental destruction, is often represented as a source of danger. Animals are suspect. They come from outside. The less they resemble us, the more the finger of suspicion points at them. They represent another, inhuman world.

Philosophical systems supported by exclusion conceive the animal as a being with a different nature to the human. This fundamental distinction starts from the idea of absolute human dignity that consists in having exclusive access to such things as logos, the good, truth, being and the like. That is why, when analyzing the question of the animal in philosophical doctrines from the pre-Socratics to the modern epoch, Simondon characterizes systems of this kind as ethical, as opposed to naturalistic ones (Simondon 2011: 55). And he is right; wherever ontological dualism appears, an ethical differentiation has already taken place. While Aristotle exposes a continuum running through all living beings, with the human still a part of the animal kingdom, in Socrates and Plato we have to do with an insuperable distance between humans and the rest of nature (13). It should be noted that while in the case of inclusion the necessarily hierarchical difference is considered as an effect of continuity (the entities range from high to low), in ethical systems, this difference is fundamental.

As Simondon points out, there is no ancient conception of the animal properly speaking, neither is there a Christian or modern conception, even though there are, of course, general features and approaches that pertain to this or that epoch (ibid.). However, according to Simondon, at any one time, philosophers, in their speculations about animals, were inclined either to a naturalist idea of continuity and affinity, like Aristotle, or to spiritualism and ethical binarism, like Socrates. It was Socrates who, in a way, invented man and, by emphasizing its radical distance from all that is natural, founded a humanism on the anthropological difference (36–37).

I would accept this definition of the two approaches as related respectively to the principle of inclusion and the principle of exclusion, but one should not forget that they are mutually presupposing and constantly pass into one another. The inclusion of the animal in the human world is the flip side of its exclusion. Before ethical and ontological dualism could appear, our moral laws had to be (unsuccessfully) imposed on animals as universal laws, and the animals had to be judged by these laws. Time and again, the beasts are banished from the human world to the wild madness of nature, and time and again, they are welcomed back. They return and try again to live among us, to observe our laws and proprieties. And each time, they fail. Consequently, the noble and all-too-human Aristotelian horses are becoming barbaric and insane Bataillean beasts, which have no place in the harmonious and proportionate universe.

It seems that, in a way, Simondon is more sympathetic towards naturalists, who insist on natural continuity (Aristotle, Montaigne), and remains critical towards spiritualists, who begin from difference (Socrates, Plato, Descartes). In turn, instead of differentiating between humans and animals, he proposes to consider the physical, the vital, the psychic and the psychosocial as levels of being understood as becoming, or as certain regimes of individuation (Simondon 1964: 153). In Simondon's ontology, there is no principal difference or border between animals and humans, but rather a general ontogenesis of flexible matter. All borders are potentially passable: 'This does not mean that there are just living beings and beings which live and think: probably, sometimes animals find themselves in a psychic situation, it is just that these situations, which lead to acts of thought, are less frequent in animals' (152).

According to Simondon, the vital, the psychic (which can also mean the subjective) and so on are not substances, but rather different modes, different possibilities of the pre-individual as a kind of potentiality, which – in case of living matter – is resumed in a certain act. Life, says Simondon, is 'the theatre of individuation' (Simondon 2009: 7).[2] Here, any living being is capable of acting, particularly when it faces some new, unfamiliar problem: 'true psychism appears when vital functions can no longer solve the problems posed to a living being' (Simondon 1964: 153) or, more generally:

> There is, in the living, an individuation *by the individual* and not only a functioning that would be the result of an individuation completed once and for all, as if it had been manufactured; the living being resolves problems, not only by adapting itself, which is to say by modifying its relation to the environment (which a machine can do), but by modifying itself, by inventing new internal structures and by introducing itself in its entirety into the axiomatic of vital problems. (Simondon 2009: 7)

Does this mean, therefore, that the animal can make a psychic or intellectual effort, can perform an act, in a case where all other available tools – claws, teeth, hoofs, wings and so on – are insufficient or ineffective? But is it not possible here to discern a familiar Aristotelian motif – the incessant desire to provide all living creatures, regardless of the level of their 'perfection', with access to the universal and reasonable order?

Trying to imagine these possible individuations, one should recall Kafka's absurdist animals, and the dramatic examples of their becoming human. The most successful is the ape that turns human in a desperate attempt to escape his narrow cage. It is not that he desired to become human, not at all. As Deleuze and Guattari put it, 'for Kafka, animal essence is the way out, the escape route, even in one place or in a cage. A way out, and not liberty. A living escape route and not an attack' (Deleuze and Guattari 1986: 35).[3] In *A Report to An Academy* the ape-man insists the following:

> No, freedom was not what I wanted. Only a way out; …
> there was no attraction for me in imitating human beings; I
> imitated them because I needed a way out, and for no other
> reason. (Kafka 1995: 253, 257)

So, the act of transformation from ape into man was not supposed to be a manifestation of free will or something similar. Rather, it was the other way around – he did not have any other options; there was no choice. To find a way out from a place that apparently does not have a way out – this is a real escape. To escape means to break out of a situation in which there is no choice:

> Until then I had had so many ways out of everything, and now
> I had none. I was pinned down. Had I been nailed down, my
> right to free movement would not have been lessened. Why
> so? Scratch your flesh raw between your toes, but you won't
> find the answer. Press yourself against the bar behind you till it
> nearly cuts you in two, you won't find the answer. I had no way
> out but I had to devise one, for without it I could not live. (253)

The whole situation of the ape, his animal body squeezed into the cage, was so unbearable, that, after numerous attempts to use his accustomed habits and skills, he – finally – tried something completely new. He 'concluded' – retrospectively – that the very fact that he was in the cage was caused by his so-called 'species-being', his being-ape, and that in order to escape he 'had to stop being an ape' (ibid.) and start to *imitate* humans, because they were the ones who were freely walking around. In this situation of impossibility he literally applied mimesis, and the 'plan' worked:

> I did not think things out, but I observed everything quietly. I watched these men go to and fro, always the same faces, the same movements, often it seemed to me there was only the same man. So this man or these men walked about unimpeded. A lofty goal faintly dawned before me. No one promised me that if I became like them the bars of my cage would be taken away. Such promises for apparently impossible contingencies are not given. But if one achieves the impossible, the promises appear later retrospectively precisely where one had looked in vain for them before … It was so easy to imitate these people. (255)

This Kafkian mimesis, which finally aims to make the animal to leave the zoo, looks so different from the Aristotelian one, which does not cause any radical individual transformation, but secures the situation when everyone and everything remains in their place. Kafka's individuations include a hunger-striking dog performing a biological experiment on itself (*Investigations of a Dog*), a nervous burrow-dweller playing with the idea of the social contract (*The Burrow*), mice as a utopian collective of music lovers (*Josephine the Singer, or the Mouse Folk*) and, of course, Dr Bucephalus, the true academic horse and formerly the battle horse of Alexander the Great, now lawyer (*The New Advocate*). Isn't becoming a lawyer a good alternative for a beast, who otherwise would have stayed outside the law, or in a cage, a prisoner of its own animality?

> So perhaps it is really best to do as Bucephalus has done and absorb oneself in law books. In the quiet lamplight, his flanks unhampered by the thighs of a rider, free and far from the clamour of battle, he reads and turns the pages of our ancient books. (415)

2

Before the law

An animal 'before the law': On which side of the gate does it stand? According to Derrida and Agamben, the animal, as well as the sovereign, is apparently outside the law. Thus, Agamben's animal can be described in terms of a bare life; that is, contrary to the human, it cannot be sacrificed, but it can simply be killed, slaughtered without ceremony. It is deprived of any right, or, better, provided with a number of rights that are as easily alienable as they are guaranteed by the very institutions of alienation. This figure is exactly the seamy side of the official ideology of rights accorded to animals and other possible 'others'. However, I would like to point out that this is not the eternal condition of animality. Long before the rights were instituted, animals were already subjected to law and animal killing in particular was widely prohibited.

The first references here are, of course, ancient totemism and prehistoric religion, in which animal killing is strictly prohibited. This prohibition is necessarily violated in a ritual transgression, animal sacrifice, in which animals have the sacral status of a patron or forefather of man. Here, they are outside the law, beyond the border of prohibition, in the ambiguity of the sacred. And here they are 'the first subject matter for painting': 'Probably the first paint was animal blood' (Berger 2009: 16).

Georges Bataille, who dedicated a number of his writings to the prehistoric, namely Palaeolithic cave paintings, draws special attention to the fact that animal representations were found in caves that cannot be considered places of constant habitation. Certain areas that are covered with drawings are clearly not easily accessible. Apparently, prehistoric painters made considerable efforts to get there and draw in darkness or in the dim light of a torch. For Bataille, such efforts could result only from a really deep affection provoked in humans by the very figure of an animal, and this feeling, he believes, was essentially religious. He insists on the idea of the religious origins of art – and of humanity itself. Bataille's favourite example is a famous rock painting in the Lascaux cave, which is 'so difficult to access that today the public is not admitted, in the bottom of a kind of pit', and which represents huge animals and a small man; the latter is wearing the mask of a beast:

A dying bison, losing its intestines, is depicted there in front of a dead man (apparently dead). Other details hardly render this strange composition intelligible. I cannot insist on it: I can only recall the childlike aspect of the image of a man; this aspect is even more striking since the dead man has the head of a bird. I do not claim to explain this celebrated mystery. None of the proposed interpretations appear satisfying to me. However, looking at it from the perspective I have just introduced, situating it in a world of religious equivocality, reached in violent reactions, I can say that this painting buried in the depths of the holiest of holies in the Lascaux cave is the measure of this world; it is even *the* measure of this world. From this moving and intelligible world from which religion emerged to the inextricable proliferation of religions. (Bataille 2009: 137)

The mask and the man with an animal head clearly refer to various aspects of totemism. The cult of the animal derives, first of all, from the evidence of its primordial kinship with humans. The Bataillean human enters the world by recognizing this kinship and at the same time negating it through the act of separation. Second, it marks the animals' primordial superiority over humans. Of course, the beast was stronger; thus, the killing of a big wild animal required the efforts of the entire collective of hunters. But this is not the only reason. Bataille emphasizes the contrast between the smallness of man and the grandeur of the animal, insisting on the idea of the *divine* nature of the animal. Animals are the first gods, and therefore cave paintings are literally the icons of the Neanderthal. Bataillean prehistoric animals are sovereign, which is why they are gods. It is important to remember that, for Bataille, sovereignty sides not so much with power, but with freedom – animals *do not work*:

These moving figurations oppose in a way the figuration of man, what we must consider the inferiority felt by primitive humanity, which worked and spoke, in front of the apparition of the silent animal, which did not work. In principle, the *human* figurations in the caves are of lesser quality, they tend toward caricature, and they are often concealed *beneath an animal mask*. Thus it seems to me that *animality* for the man in the painted caves – and for archaic hunters of our day – was closer to a religious aspect, which later came to correspond to the name 'divinity'. (140)

Compared to a primitive cave painter,[1] the contemporary artist cannot but fake this initial impulse towards sacrifice. Thus, among others, Hermann Nitsch, who 'defines himself not as an artist but rather as a priest working with the basics of all religions and searching for a new basis for the religious feeling in the contemporary world' (Chernoba 2012), persistently imitates animal sacrifice in his theatrical performances in the 1960s.

The problem with that is not, however, that Nitsch performs a fake sacrifice, as compared to some real sacrifice practised by the primitives. In a way, every sacrifice is fake or, as Bataille would put it, a simulacrum, or a spectacle, given that the subject of sacrifice basically replaces himself with the animal-object (in the case of animal sacrifice), because this is the way to go beyond the limit of death, while staying alive. Let us avoid this notoriously overdiscussed issue of the difference between the fake and the real, the inauthentic and the authentic, as if (which always risks suggesting that) in earlier times everything was 'for real' and now we are merely dealing with pale imitations.

As noted by David Kilpatrick, among the charges against Nitsch were 'accusations of animal killing, though, in keeping with the Manifesto of 1962, Nitsch only used animals that had already died of old age or had to be put down' (Kilpatrick 2008: 59), which 'raises a significant obstacle to the full realization of what he came to term "the primal excess": since the corpses that were employed were already dead, the most powerful element of the sacrificial rite was missing, the death of the other' (Kilpatrick 2008: 59). Thus, Nitsch sacrifices European farm animals, bought at slaughterhouses. These animals were already dead before facing their second death in the artwork.

Is it possible to qualify the killing of the dead as a sacrifice? Juridically, no: one cannot sacrifice what is not sacred; it can simply be slaughtered. The status of the animal in contemporary society does not correspond to the idea of sacrifice. While traditional sacrificial rituals are based on the transgression, violation of a prohibition – first of all, a prohibition to kill someone or something which represents a sacred value for the members of a given community – here there is no prohibition to transgress. According to the law, the killing of this kind of lamb is not prohibited: its life is not sacred but bare. It is dwelling in a grey zone, in-between life and death. This zone is populated by undead animals, which can be slaughtered multiple times. Drawn into this carousel, it never stops dying. The slaughter as an infinite loop.

In his discussion of the mythopoietic aspects of sacrifice from Nietzsche to Nitsch by way of Bataille, who locates sacrifice at the very basis of his philosophy, Kilpatrick emphasizes the decontextualized character of this artistic gesture, which is looking for a new religion. Admittedly, putting the three figures together makes sense, for Bataille, too, was trying to reconstitute some premises for religious experience in our non-religious, 'profane' world. As if there and then, in days of yore, the first people experienced some intensity of the real, which we, in this day and age, lack or perceive ourselves to have lost. And there was a period (when he established the journal, and the secret community, *Acephale*, from 1936 to 1939) during which Bataille honestly intended to retrieve religion by way of the ritual.

It is true that it is not without nostalgia that Bataille refers to prehistoric times. However, a nostalgic utopia of authenticity or the primordial community of people is not Bataille's most radical mistake or fault, as critics like Jean-Luc Nancy would argue (Nancy 1991a). In fact, his fascination with the primitive, which has provoked much antagonism among contemporary thinkers, did not significantly affect his overall critical impact. It is just a style of thought, which does not necessarily feel nostalgia for a bygone age, but which always tends to attribute a feeling of immediacy or naivety to a more or less remote past. Bataille was convinced that the Neanderthal really believed in his animal gods, and Nancy believed that Bataille was so naïve as to really believe in the naivety of the Neanderthal. Similarly to that, as Slavoj Žižek puts it, Derrida believes in the phallogocentrism of the philosophers of the past who were so naïve as to believe in the omnipotence of reason:

Viewed through the lenses of modern Western 'rational' thought taken as the standard of maturity, its Other cannot but appear as 'primitives' trapped in magic thinking, 'really believing' that their tribe originates from their totemic animal, that a pregnant woman has been inseminated by a spirit and not by a man, etc. Rational thought thus engenders the figure of 'irrational' mythical thought – what we get here is (again) the process of violent simplification (reduction, obliteration) which occurs with the rise of the New: in order to assert something radically New, the entire past, with all its inconsistencies, has to be reduced to some basic defining feature ('metaphysics', 'mythical thought', 'ideology' …). Derrida himself enacts the same simplification in his deconstructive mode: all the past is totalized as 'phallogocentrism' or 'metaphysics of presence'. (Žižek 2012: 409)

This tendency is also called projection. Bataille projects the naivety of the sacrifice onto savage man, the naivety of the closed system of Absolute knowledge onto Hegel and the naivety of immanence onto animals. Nancy projects the naivety of projection onto Bataille. But, I insist, this is not an obstacle, or, at least, this is not what is of most interest here: projection is rather one of philosophy's numerous bad habits and symptoms. Is there any other way of dealing with the history of philosophy?

After all, in this case, the issue with Bataille is not that he projected religion onto primitives, but rather that he did not see religion in the present time. One could say that the myth shared by Nitsch and Bataille is the myth of the absence of myth, the myth of the present time deprived of the sacred. In spite of all the efforts of the conjoined forces of the Enlightenment, rationalism and capitalism, modernity did not manage in the end to secularize human society and disenchant the world. Both religion and myth still exist, as do rituals and beliefs. Thus, according to Walter Benjamin, capitalism is a religion. Capitalism is 'not only a religiously conditioned construction, as Weber thought, but an essentially religious phenomenon' (Benjamin 2004: 259–263). We are not living in a non-religious society; it is just that the essence of religion has changed. And – what is most important here – the animal has lost its central (sacred and sacrificial) place within it. This fact, however, was quite clear to Bataille, who emphasizes 'the passage from the initial opposition between *animality-divinity* and *humanity* to the opposition that still prevails today, that reigns over even minds foreign to all religion, between *animality* devoid of any religious signification and *humanity-divinity*?' (Bataille 2009: 141–142).

The status of animals has changed. After prehistory, they are no longer gods. Yet, the traces of their kinship with god and man have never fully disappeared; thus, the Greeks shared with them their cosmos, and in the Middle Ages animals still lived in the same universe as man, namely the universe of God's creation.

In contrast to prehistoric art, where man is depicted under the mask of a beast, in the galaxy of mediaeval and Renaissance painting, animals, even in bestiaries, often have human faces. And not only animals – children have them too. To be more precise, in the world of the Creature, made after the image of God and in His likeness, one can see only numerous variations of one and the same face. The singularity and the uniqueness of the mediaeval image correspond to the universality and sameness of the God.

In turn, as a result of god's presence in every element of his creation, mediaeval law did not apply only to human beings. The medieval legal system extended to animals, too. If in totemism animals could be sacrificed, then in the Europe of the Middle Ages, it was possible to execute or excommunicate them. Animals were put on trial. This means that they were considered to be conscious of what they were doing and held responsible for every 'crime' they committed and for all of the damage that they inflicted. Formally, they were given almost the same juridical status as humans.

Nowadays, people are bewildered by the idea of trying animals according to human law. Yet, in a way, today's juridical attitude towards animals no longer focuses on their responsibilities, but on their rights, thus drifting towards a new form of inclusion that, paradoxically, refers back to the dimension of the animal-in-law of older times. It is as if, after a long period of excluding the non-human animal from the enlightened and rationalized world, where they were legally treated as things (no moral conviction here, just a statement of a juridical fact), we, contemporary humans, cannot wait to return to the shared universe and to welcome them back again.

Animal trials are not, of course, an exclusively mediaeval phenomenon. They existed in earlier periods and persist beyond the Middle Ages (they are still taking place in this day and age, although they are quite rare). Jen Girgen, who dedicated an extended article to animal prosecution, mentions, among other things, an analogous practice in ancient Greece, about which we know relatively little:

In fact, there is no direct evidence that any such trials actually occurred. However, by most accounts, the primary purpose of the prosecution of animals would have been the same one that governed the Greeks' prosecution of inanimate objects: removal of the pollution that, because of the crime, had 'contaminated' the community. Following the trial, if the finders of fact and law declared the offending animal guilty, the animal was likely executed. Her corpse would then be 'cast beyond the border' to rid the land of pollution. (Girgen 2003: 105–106)

One of the evidences is found in Plato:

If a beast of draught or other animal cause homicide, except in the case when the deed is done by a beast competing in one of the public sports, the kinsmen shall institute proceedings for homicide against the slayer; [and] on conviction, the beast shall be put to death and cast out beyond the frontier. (Plato 1934: 263–264)

The Greek idea of an animal trial is not so much about punishment as about clearing away pollution, maintaining the frontier of a community. Within this frontier, a community is safe and pure. Whatever created trouble should be cast out. Not because it had committed a crime, but rather because it had caused misfortune. According to Walter Hyde, the Greeks believe 'that the moral equilibrium of the community had been disturbed by the murder and that somebody or something must be punished or else dire misfortune, in the form of plagues,

droughts, reverses in men's fortunes, would overtake the land'
(Hyde 1916: 698).

By ridding itself of these elements, the Greek cosmos aims to
restore its frail balance. In turn, the mediaeval universe is run
according to the law, which is not in the least like the blind will
of the gods. Christian law is known; it is given to people, and it
is supposed to be understood and carefully observed. But even
a deep respect for moral law does not liberate one from guilt,
because, as we know, in the beginning there was sin.

According to Girgen, mediaeval Europe knew, generally
speaking, two kinds of animal trials, both carried out in almost
the same way as human trials. Secular tribunals 'typically
hosted trials involving individual domesticated animals' or
tried and punished animals which 'caused physical injury or
death to a human being', whereas ecclesiastical tribunals tended
to have jurisdiction 'over groups of untamed animals, such as
swarms of insects' or animals which 'caused a public nuisance
(typically involving the destruction of crops intended for human
consumption)'. Animals that were tried individually included
pigs, cows, bulls, horses, mules, oxen, goats, sheep and dogs.
Ecclesiastical trials mostly applied to moles, mice, rats, snakes,
birds, snails, worms, grasshoppers, caterpillars, termites, various
types of beetles and flies, other unspecified insects and 'vermin'
and even eels and dolphins (Girgen 2003: 99).

In spite of their non-traditional defendants, both the
ecclesiastical and secular courts took these proceedings
very seriously and strictly adhered to the legal customs and

formal procedural rules that had been established for human criminal defendants. The community, at its own expense, provided the accused animals with defence counsel, and these lawyers raised complex legal arguments on behalf of the animal defendants. In criminal trials, animal defendants were sometimes detained in jail alongside human prisoners. Evidence was weighed and judgement decreed as though the defendant were human. Finally, in the secular court, when the time came to carry out the punishment (usually lethal), the court procured the services of a professional hangman, who was paid in a like manner as for the other, more traditional, executions he performed. (ibid.)

Following execution, animals were usually buried, or hanged, or decapitated. Thus, among numerous stories, Edward Payson Evans, who documented more than 191 persecutions and excommunications of animals between the IX and XX centuries, recounts the following:

> In 1386, the tribunal of Falaise sentenced a sow to be mangled and maimed in the head and forelegs, and then to be hanged, for having torn the face and arms of a child and thus caused its death. … As if to make the travesty of justice complete, the sow was dressed in man's clothes and executed on the public square near the city hall at an expense to the state of ten sous and ten deniers, besides a pair of gloves to the hangman. (Evans 1906: 140)

However, animal trials did not necessarily end up imposing the death penalty. In Austria, in 1712, a dog reportedly bit a member of the municipal council in the leg. The dog was tried and sentenced to one year in the *Narrenkötterlein*, which was 'a sort of pillory or iron cage standing in the market-place, in which blasphemers, evil-livers, rowdies and other peace-breakers were commonly confined' (Evans 1906: 175).

In spite of significant ideological differences in the Greek and mediaeval approaches to animal trials, they have something in common, and I would certainly agree with Girgen, who tends to explain this common attitude in terms of 'order'. I emphasized this term earlier on, and I would like to insist on it, as far as it makes sense when discussing animals that are running back and forth through the borders and gates of the law:

> Those theories focusing on order and control are particularly helpful to an understanding of the motives behind the trials. Greeks and mediaeval Europeans, it is suggested, originally held these trials to establish cognitive control over a disorderly world ... In other words, the animal trials were derived from a search for order. People needed to believe that the natural universe was lawful, even when certain events, such as a pig killing a human child, seemed to defy all reasonable explanation. So they turned to the courts. (Girgen 2003: 119)

I have already mentioned Dr Bucephalus, a character in Kafka's *The New Advocate*. No doubt the figure of the animal-lawyer is fantastical, but some human advocates of animals were actually part of the mediaeval legal system. As noted by Esther Cohen, they 'took their job very seriously, devoting a great deal of time, knowledge and legal experience to the defence of their clients' (Cohen 1986: 123).

> One of the most renowned of these animal public defenders was Bartholomew Chassenée, who would later become the first president of the Parlement de Provence (a position corresponding to Chief Justice) and a significant contributor to the evolution of sixteenth-century French legal thought. In 1522, in a case that would help establish him as an eminent legal scholar, Chassenée was appointed to defend the rats of Autun, who had been accused of destroying the province's barley crop. In defence of his clients' failure to appear before the court in response to its formal summons, Chassenée first argued that because his clients lived in different locations in several villages, a single summons would fail to notify them all of the complaint. The court agreed, and a second citation was read in all the parishes inhabited by the rats. When the rats still did not appear after this second summons, Chassenée explained that the disobedience was now due to the length and difficulty of the journey; he argued further that it was the rats' fear of the cats they would encounter on their journey that kept them from their obligation. (Girgen 2003: 101–102)

However, these arguments in defence of animals on trial did not exhaust the entire field of animal advocacy discourse. As human thought developed over time, they became more and more general, rationalized and refined. Lawyers, the animal defence counsels, among others, stood at the origins of humanistic discourse. Their principal argument now sounds banal, but at the time, it was revolutionary. The argument was that one could not try animals because they do not have an intellect, and this can be interpreted as a considerable step towards modern rationality. The paradox is that it was precisely this humanism that became the basis for the future treatment of animals as things, for excluding them from the human universe because they lack human dignity, intellect or other particularly human merits. This type of argument was based on the idea of human superiority, inherent in classical humanist tradition. Advocates of animals established to the satisfaction of the court that we could not charge animals because we cannot speak to them, because they do not understand us, they do not know the law and are alien to it.

3

The insane

There was also another mediaeval argument presented in the animals' favour. According to this argument, animals are innocent. Here we are dealing with the ambiguity of Christian tradition. On the one hand, this tradition is distressed by the sinfulness of the animal nature of man. On the other, it admires the innocence of the beast that does not know the difference between good and evil, the bestial naivety and innocence from which we have to learn. What if this tender feeling towards the holy simplicity of God's creatures is one of the signs, so diverse in Christianity, of the pagan worship of nature? Worship that, according to the Christian theologian G.K. Chesterton, already contained the seeds of an understanding of its own 'fallacy'. For Chesterton, pagan civilization was not simply a very high one, but 'the highest that humanity ever reached', for this civilization, besides its own 'arts of poetry and plastic representation', 'political ideals', 'system of logic and language', discovered 'its own mistake':

That mistake was too deep to be ideally defined; the short-hand of it is to call it the mistake of nature-worship. It might almost as truly be called the mistake of being natural; and it was a very natural mistake … The wisest man in the world set out to be natural; and the most unnatural thing in the world was the very first thing they did. The immediate effect of saluting the sun and the sunny sanity of nature was a perversion spreading like a pestilence … It was the discovery of that deeper thing, humanly speaking, that constituted the conversion to Christianity. There is a bias in man like the bias on a bowl; and Christianity was the discovery of how to correct the bias and therefore hit the mark. There are many who will smile at the saying; but it is profoundly true to say that the glad good news brought by the Gospel was the news of original sin. (Chesterton 2011: 11–12)

Unlike Christian people, mediaeval animals were innocent. They were unaware of sin, good and evil. They never left nature, or, rather, they had never left the Kingdom of Heaven.[1] But if animals were unaware of sin, then they were unaware of the Christian message, the Gospel. One recalls the aspiration of St. Francis of Assisi to talk to them and teach them. The saint really tried his best to give them access to the universal divine law. He was preaching the Word of God to beasts and birds, and the success of his preaching depended on how nearly he could approximate their innocence.

Legend has it that St. Francis even managed to convert Brother Wolf, who was first bad and then became good. Animals gathered around the priest, listening to him, asking questions – each in their own language – in order to praise God afterwards. In this glorification, every living being, be it a monster, 'shapeless or dumb or merely destructive', finds its sense, as part of the new unity of the Christian faith, which makes its way through the abyss at the heart of the cracked world:

> It is also true that he sees more of the things themselves when he sees more of their origin; for their origin is a part of them and indeed the most important part of them. Thus they become more extraordinary by being explained. He has more wonder at them but less fear of them; for a thing is really wonderful when it is significant and not when it is insignificant; and a monster, shapeless or dumb or merely destructive, may be larger than the mountains, but is still in a literal sense insignificant. For a mystic like St. Francis the monsters had a meaning; that is, they had delivered their message. They spoke no longer in an unknown tongue. That is the meaning of all those stories whether legendary or historical, in which he appears as a magician speaking the language of beasts and birds. (40)

In order to speak to beasts and birds, it was necessary to pass through a difficult process of purification, to get rid of all the external influence and first become poor like they were. Preaching to animals, which opened the door to a pious life, was possible during an era in which poverty and misery were qualified not as vice or crime, but rather the opposite, as a sign of sanctity. It was as if poverty could open up the possibility of communication, the basis for a proper social existence, in which even wolves could be included as brothers. Franciscan belief presupposed a kind of utopia of poverty, essential for a genuine Christian community. As if there was a kind of power in misery as opposed to the misery of power, reflected by worldly wealth and gold, exercised by the Church or the State.

It is no surprise that such utopian ideas were picked up by contemporary thinkers, like Giorgio Agamben, who claim that the West must return to Franciscanism, which teaches 'to think life as that which is never given as property but only as a common use' (Agamben 2013: xiii),[2] and Michael Hardt and Antonio Negri, who 'further radicalise the reversibility of Agamben's transformation of "bare life" into a resource of transcendence by treating this "bareness" or "nudity" as an enriching power' (Noys 2011). Here is a famous passage from their *Empire*:

> There is an ancient legend that might serve to illuminate the future life of communist militancy: that of Saint Francis of Assisi. Consider his work. To denounce the poverty of the multitude he adopted that common condition and discovered there the ontological power of a new society. The communist militant does the same, identifying in the common condition of the multitude its enormous wealth. Francis in opposition to nascent capitalism refused every instrumental discipline, and in opposition to the mortification of the flesh (in poverty and in the constituted order) he posed as a joyous life, including all of being and nature, the animals, sister moon, brother sun,

the birds of the field, the poor and exploited humans, together against the will of power and corruption. Once again in postmodernity we find ourselves in Francis's situation, posing against the misery of power the joy of being. This is a revolution that no power will control – because biopower and communism, cooperation and revolution remain together, in love, simplicity, and also innocence. This is the irrepressible lightness and joy of being communist. (Hardt and Negri 2000: 413)

Sometime later, after having adopted Max Weber's definition of the spirit of capitalism, virtue and access to the good, universal and individual, become literally measured by property and labour. And then again animals, being both poor and non-working (unemployed), are already outside the law. Now their place is next to the lower classes and to society's outcasts.

In the first part of *History of Madness*, Michel Foucault describes how in the course of the Reformation, with the rise of the moral value of work, idleness starts to be exposed to blame, and poverty loses its halo of sanctity and gets treated as a crime against the bourgeois order:

A new form of pathos came into being, which no longer spoke of a glorification of pain, not of salvation proper both to Charity and to Poverty, but concerned rather the idea of civic duty, and showed the poor and destitute to be both a consequence of disorder and an obstacle to order. The aim therefore was no longer to glorify poverty in the act of relieving it, but quite simply to dispose of it altogether ... Poverty is no longer a part of a dialectic of humiliation and glorification but rather of the relationship of disorder to order and is now locked in guilt. After Calvin and Luther, poverty bore the marks of an immemorial punishment, and became, in the world of state-assisted charity, self-complacency and crime against the good order of the state. From being the object of a religious experience and sanctified, poverty became the object of a moral conception that condemned it. The great houses of confinement were a clear result of that evolution. (Foucault 2006: 57)

According to this prior order, a strange man such as Francis of Assisi would be treated not as a saint, but as mad, and he might easily have found himself in a detention centre together with beggars and vagabonds, because, as Foucault would put it, the mad 'crossed the frontiers of the bourgeois order, and become alien to the sacred limits of its ethics' (Foucault 2006: 72).

The madman, who, from the point of view of the mediaeval idea of charity, still emanated something of the secret power of misery, is no longer a messenger of the sacred world, crowned with this very misery. He is descending to a hell of turbulent animality, the tumult of which could be more frightening than leprosy for the nascent reasonable order. It is certainly far from random that the former leper colony now becomes a new shelter for the insane.

Foucault notes that in the Classical Age the figure of the madman combines criminal poverty and idleness with the animal, inhuman principle. People of this era consider that the human is the one who thinks. The one who does not think is not human. Madness reveals the absurdity of the animal nature of man in all the monstrosity of its agony, its sickness, but, simultaneously, its freedom. Foucault places madness as a direct relation between man and his animality:

> The negative fact that 'the mad were not treated as human beings' was the result of a very real thought process, in that this apparently inhuman indifference betrayed a deep-seated worry which since antiquity, and above all since the Middle Ages, had given the animal world its familiar strangeness, its menacing marvels, and the weight of all the fears it inspires. Yet this animal fear that accompanied the perception of madness with all its imaginary landscapes no longer had the meaning that it had had for previous centuries. Metamorphosis into an animal was no longer an indication of the power of the devil, nor a result of the diabolical alchemy of unreason. The animal in man was no longer the indicator of a beyond, but had become in itself his madness, with no reference to anything other than itself, his madness in a natural state. (148)

In particular, the places of isolation, or confinement, where madmen are placed for their correction, are arranged similarly to menageries. The purpose of isolation is to secure classical reason against madness, the social order against the outburst of poverty and the human being against the animal, who now bears no resemblance to the human.

Foucault explains that the phenomenon of the exclusion of madness (in the form of isolation) should be interpreted as a 'police matter', which cannot but remind us of Bataillean 'police regulations' governing the classical Greek against the barbarism of the 'criminal classes'. Why, however, does one need the police? Which kind of order should be secured? Foucault directly associates the need for police regulations with the necessity of forced labour. Both the madman and the indigent do not work, and I must add here: animals, too, do not work.[3]

> Confinement, the signs of which are to be found massively across Europe throughout the seventeenth century, was a 'police' matter. In the classical age the word had a meaning that was quite precise, referring to a bundle of measures that made work possible and necessary to all those who could not possibly live without it. Voltaire was soon to formulate the question, but Colbert's contemporaries had voiced it already: 'What? Now you are set up as a body of people, but you still haven't found a way to force the rich to make the poor work? Evidently, you haven't even reached the first principles of the "police"'. (62)

But besides that, first of all, one needs a police force for oneself, in order to secure oneself against this animality or madness, which could derive from the very interior of the rational human (qua rational animal). The Classical Age tends to turn this danger into an impossibility; it considers insanity as a social matter, which can approach from the insecure space of an outside. Social practices of confinement are accompanied by the theoretical impact of the police of the Classical Age, which is represented by Cartesian rationalist metaphysics, or, as Foucault puts it, Cartesian exclusion. Foucault refers to Descartes, who could put everything in doubt except his own thought. In order to establish a true and certain foundation of knowledge, Descartes lists the main forms of delusion and illusion: of the senses and sensible perception, of madness and so on. Finally, he takes into account the hypothesis that all that we see is not reality, but a dream or a trick played by the evil genius, God-the-trickster. But even if all we see is an illusion, even if everything is doubtful, there is no doubt that I, myself, think, and this is the certainty of the *cogito*, which is, according to Foucault, based on the exclusion of madness.

It is precisely non-thinking that differentiates the thinking subject, fully confident in the certainty of his *cogito*, from the insane, who are totally alien to truth: 'I, when I think, cannot be considered insane' (45). I would add, however, that the animal in the Cartesian system is a being even more alien to the human than the insane, for from the mouth of the insane one can hear something like human speech, but from the mouth of an animal – never:

Now in just these two ways we can also know the difference between man and beast. For it is quite remarkable that there are no man so dull-witted or stupid – and this includes even madmen – that they are incapable of arranging various words together and forming an utterance from them in order to make theirs thoughts understood; whereas there is no other animal, however perfect and well-endowed it may be, that can do the like. This does not happen because they lack the necessary organs, for we see that magpies and parrots can utter words as we do, and yet they cannot speak as we do:

that is, they cannot show that they are thinking what they are saying. On the other hand, men born deaf and dumb, and thus deprived of speech organs as much as the beasts or even more so, normally invent their own signs to make themselves understood by those who, being regularly in their company, have the time to learn their language. This shows not merely that the beasts have less reason than men, but that they have no reason at all. (Descartes 1985, 1: 140)

Descartes' animal is incapable not only of thinking but also of feeling. It doesn't have an intelligent soul and can thus neither think nor suffer. That is why it can easily be used, without reservations of a moral or any other kind, as an object for scientific experimentation:

> Indeed, in several places Descartes describes with enthusiasm his own forays into vivisection. In a letter to Plemp, Descartes notes that the hearts of fish, 'after they had been cut out, go on beating for much longer than the heart of any terrestrial animal'; he goes on to explain how he has refuted a view of Galen's concerning the functioning of cardiac arteries by having 'opened the chest of a live rabbit and removed the ribs to expose the heart and the trunk of the aorta … Continuing the vivisection, I cut away half the heart'. (Waldau and Patton 2006: 123)

In his *Description of the Human Body*, Descartes shares the results of 'a very striking experiment':

> If you slice off the pointed end of the heart in a live dog, and insert a finger into one of the cavities, you will feel

unmistakably that every time the heart gets shorter it presses the finger, and every time it gets longer it stops pressing it. (Descartes 1985, 1: 317)

The heart of a dog will not last long at Descartes' anatomical table. The life of this perhaps stray animal, as well as the life of any other Cartesian animal, does not endure beyond the moment at which blood ceases to circulate through the arteries. Those animals are almost already dead, or rather undead, and, incidentally, one might say, that a passage from life to death, their short stay in the grey zone in between, is an object of scientific and aesthetic inspiration in the Classical Age.

In fact, when talking about Cartesian animals, the words 'life' or 'death' are not really relevant. Through his experimentation, the scientist is just trying to investigate the workings of the machine called the body. Basically, the animal body is a machine of the same kind as the human body. By understanding the functioning of the former, we comprehend the functioning of the latter. In Descartes' mechanical universe, animals move as automata, adapted for this or that kind of operation. As he explains, the fact that they show some good skills,

proves rather that they have no intelligence at all, and that it is nature which acts in them according to the disposition of their organs. In the same way a clock, consisted only of wheels and springs, can count the hours and measure the time more accurately than we can with all our wisdom. (141)

But in that case, what differentiates the human body from the animal machine? It is the mind or the soul, the immortal soul, which actually brings the human body to life. It is situated in a little gland at the centre of the brain, the 'pineal gland'. But what brings all the sensations to the pineal gland, making this body truly human, that is, a truly living body, as opposed to a machine or a mere corpse, which cannot feel? It is those tiny fibres, brain pores, called 'animal spirits'. Animal spirits flow through nerves and muscles between the brain and the extremities of the body, imparting human sensations – pain, desire and passions.

By explaining the animal as a machine, which does not have real sensations, does not desire or suffer, but just reacts as a complex *automaton*, consisting of bones, muscles and organs, one could also attempt to easily explain its behaviour and to assume its activity is predictable (if known very well), and thus protect oneself from a sudden intrusion and immediate spontaneous aggression, or to neutralize it. In the bourgeois comfort of the rational Cartesian world ('I am here, sitting by the fire, wearing a winter dressing-gown, holding this piece of paper in my hands, and so on …' (Descartes 1985, 2: 13)), animals are not allowed; neither a prudent Aristotelian swallow nor a blessed bird of St. Francis will fly in.

However, there is no more easy and at the same time thankless task than criticizing Descartes for his maltreatment of animals. There is, indeed, a Descartes of the world of *cogito* supposedly pure and free of both insanity and animality. But there is another Descartes, the one who, as Žižek puts it, 'himself misunderstood the *cogito* in his illegitimate passage from *cogito* to *res cogitans*', for '*cogito* is not a separate substance different from the body' (Žižek 2012: 408), the Descartes of the potential passage from radical doubt to the radical split: 'This split, repressed by the *cogito*, re-emerges with Freud' (Chiesa 2011). This Descartes, one might say, truly experiences madness (but also animality) as impossibility – in so far as he is not indifferent to it, he cannot just coexist with it, accepting it with equanimity.

On the one hand, he might experience it as something excluded, something which is beyond the frontier of reason and which surrounds his rational universe, not simply threatening it from the outside but actively constituting the very inside of subjectivity by excluding its double, which is insane. This is Foucault's point: madness, as well as reason itself, is a certain function of power relations and a historically determined discursive construct. Instead of confronting madness, Descartes tries to avoid it by means of the *cogito*, and – in the last instance – by soliciting a guarantee from God: as Lacan points out in different places, Cartesian doubt draws its force from this ultimate trust in a 'big Other'; *cogito* avoids being left alone by throwing itself at the mercy of the divine.

On the other hand, he experiences it as something truly internal. This would be Derrida's argument in his famous polemic against Foucault, where he states that philosophy itself 'is perhaps the reassurance given against the anguish of being mad at the point of greatest proximity to madness' (Derrida 1978: 59). Žižek perfectly explains Derrida's position at this point in the discussion:

> In his reading of *Histoire de la folie*, Derrida focused on these four pages on Descartes which, for him, provided the

key to the entire book. Through a detailed analysis, he tries to demonstrate that, far from excluding madness, Descartes pushes it to an extreme: universal doubt, where I suspect that the entire world is an illusion, is the greatest madness imaginable. Out of this universal doubt the *cogito* emerges: even if everything is an illusion, I can still be sure that I think. Madness is thus not excluded by the *cogito*: it is not that the *cogito* is not mad, but the *cogito is true even if I am totally mad.* (Žižek 2012: 329)

This hyperbolic moment of madness is internal to philosophy and grounds it, but, just like an animal, it is being 'domesticated' and subjugated by the 'image of man as thinking substance': 'of course, every philosophy tries to control this excess, to repress it – but in repressing it, it represses its own innermost foundation' (ibid.).

There is a certain asymmetry, of course, between *exclusion* as the effect of a historically determined ensemble of social practices and discursive procedures, on the one hand, and the *repression* that denotes rather a universal political operation and the subjective experience of the unconscious. But, in a way, these contending approaches are both right; from our perspective, they even supplement each other. One can take a step further by introducing a third position, that of Lacan, in which Descartes will be, in a way, 'rehabilitated' through Freud. According to Lacan, *ego* and *cogito* do not coincide; subject is not ego, subject is unconscious, but it still thinks:

Descartes did not know, except that it involved the subject of a certainty and the rejection of all previous knowledge – but we know, thanks to Freud, that the subject of the unconscious manifests itself; that it thinks before it attains certainty. (Lacan 1998: 37)

I would like to pay attention to the fact that there is an idea lurking behind this formula: 'Descartes did not know ... but *we* know' – the idea that both in Descartes and in Freud (but also in Lacan) we are dealing with the same subject. Before the appearance of any *I, it* thinks. As Mladen Dolar says in his article, devoted to Lacan's approach to *cogito*,

Lacan largely defined his project with the slogan announcing 'a return to Freud', but subsequently it turned out that this slogan has to be complemented with a corollary: the return to Freud had to pass by way of a return to Descartes. So there is a huge gap that separates Lacan from the rest of the structuralist generation, which defined itself as basically anti-Cartesian. (Žižek 1998: 14)

If, then, taking the *cogito* as the subject of the unconscious, we went back to *Civilization and Its Discontents*, where Freud presents his theory of 'organic repression', and if we take up his alignment – which goes through the processes of rejection and negation – of the unconscious with animality,[4] we'll see a true Cartesian animal, hidden somewhere in the very depths of the *cogito*.

As Carrie Rohman, who analyses the discourse of animality in modern literature, nicely puts it, 'Freud's narrative suggests that an attempted rejection of humanity's own animality created the human unconscious' (Rohman 2009: 23). For Freud, the evolutionary process finds its reflection in the development of the human individual, and the successive processes of the child becoming an adult pass through the overcoming of the animal and the erasure of its traces. Nothing sounds more obvious and simple than that now, but it is very important to note that the animality thus 'overcome', or 'rejected' or 'repressed' is not something which naively pre-existed organic repression, but something which emerges retrospectively as a result of this process. The Freudian individual is always already human who produces the entire set of projections of what he was not but at the same time of what he *was* before (the animal which is repressed by the human emerges together with this repression).

In his *Interpretation of Dreams* Freud suggests that there is a process of interpretation, which is taking place in the dream-work, where the unconscious itself is trying to erase its own traces, to fill in the gaps in the fabric of meaning, to already interpret the dream within the dream itself before any possible interpretation. And if, talking about Lacan and Descartes, Mladen Dolar introduces the figure of the *cogito* as the subject of the unconscious, then in his other work, dedicated to Hegel and Freud, he speaks about 'an unconscious philosopher, lurking in the midst of the dream', who is trying, but cannot fully manage 'to cover up his traces, he always lets the cat out of the bag, at least part of the cat' (Dolar 2012).

4

Insecure, anxious and unhappy

As well as Descartes, Hegel, indeed, is a great figure of this philosophical tradition, to which we are compelled to refer again and again and within which animals are the object of the abovementioned notorious disregard called anthropocentrism. In many ways, some works dedicated to animality in Hegel emphasize this precise moment of human superiority over animals.

Andrew Benjamin thus pursues Hegel's anthropocentrism by investigating the question of disease, as it appears in the *Philosophy of Nature*, and, through the problematic of the Other, shows how this problematic is connected, in a very complicated way, to racism and anti-Semitism (Benjamin 2007a: 61–77). For Hegel, disease is the weakness of the power of a concept, since a concept maintains the unity of a subject, and disease is what threatens this unity and can destroy it through the enlargement of some particularity. In this sense, animals are essentially weak because they live in an environment full of danger and (unlike humans) cannot really oppose to this dangerous reality with a certain power of self-constituting unity. Benjamin emphasizes that Jews in Hegel, with their religion and tradition, are also a particularity within the human species, which should be overcome in favour of the whole of humanity.[1]

To take another example, Elisabeth de Fontenay marks out two contradictory tendencies in the Hegelian discourse on animality. The first one, which she sums up briefly in one paragraph, is associated with the phenomenological tradition of regarding any living organism as a subjectivity, which, 'through the exterior processes, always maintains a unity in itself' (de Fontenay 1998: 533). The second, to which she dedicates an entire chapter entitled 'The mouth is without spirit', is the idealistic disregard towards animals. This second tendency is mostly expressed in the *Aesthetics*, where Hegel speculates about the deficiency of natural beauty. The beauty of the animal is insufficient, for it does not reach the Ideal, which is a concrete unity not only *in itself*, but also *for itself* and for others:

> But however far even animal life, as the summit of natural beauty, expresses possession of soul, nevertheless every animal life is throughout restricted and tied down to entirely specific qualities. The sphere of its existence is narrow and its interests are dominated by the natural needs of nourishment, sex etc. Its soul-life, as what is inner and what gains expression in its outward shape, is poor, abstract and worthless. Further, this inner does not emerge into appearance as *inner*; the

living thing in nature does not reveal its soul for itself, for the thing in nature is just this, that its soul remains purely inward, i.e. does not express itself as something ideal. The soul of the animal, that is to say, is, as we have just indicated, not *present to itself* as this ideal unity; if it were, then it would also *manifest* itself to others in this self-awareness. Only the self-conscious *ego* is the simple ideal which, as ideal in its own eyes, knows itself as this simple unity and therefore gives itself a reality which is no mere external, sensuous, and bodily reality, but itself one of an ideal kind. (Hegel 1998: 132)

One could say that, therefore, from an aesthetic point of view, the problem of Hegelian animals is that they are not beautiful enough. Their interior remains immediate, imprisoned inside their body, secret, concealed or hidden (the idea of the secretness of the animal will later be developed by Heidegger, who proposes *openness* as a criterion of differentiation between human beings and merely living beings). In Hegel, we see only the exterior of the animal body. And here, on the exterior level, the distinction between animals and humans can be fixed with regard to some basic aspects, which I will now enumerate with reference to Hegel's text.

First of all, we see the animal body covered with scales, wool, feathers and so on. And all those scales, wool and feathers indicate, according to Hegel, a certain *underdevelopment of the skin*. Skin is important: the stronger and purer the skin, the more beautiful the creature. The development of skin, getting rid of natural coverings and protections, accompanies an increasing spirituality, which is becoming open. Paradoxically enough, in this respect, in his *Philosophy of Nature* males bear more animal traces than females

> In mammals, the skin continues its growth into wool, hair, bristles, spines (in the hedgehog), and even into scales and armour (in the armadillo). Man, on the other hand, has a skin which is smooth, pure and much more animalized and which also sheds anything of an osseous nature. Woman has a more luxuriant head of hair. In the male, an abundance of hair on the chest and elsewhere is regarded as a sign of strength; it is, however, a relative weakness of the cutaneous organization. (Hegel 2007: 426)

But much more than skin, the *eyes* attest to the appearance of the spirit. Only in human beings does the function of the eye, through which the soul manifests itself, dominate over regular natural functions; in animals, the main part of the body is the protrusive *mouth*. This is what differentiates a human *face*[2] from an animal head, in which 'the predominant thing is the mouth, as the tool for chewing, with the upper and lower jaw, the teeth, and the masticatory muscles'. All other organs are only 'servants and helpers' of the mouth: 'the nose especially as sniffing out food, the eyes, less important, for spying it'.

> The express prominence of these formations exclusively devoted to natural needs and their satisfaction gives the animal head the appearance of being merely adapted to natural functions and without any spiritual ideal significance. So, after all, we can understand the whole of the animal organism in the light

of these tools in the mouth. In other words, the specific kind of food demands a specific structure of the mouth, a special kind of teeth, with which there then most closely correspond the build of the jaws, masticatory muscles, cheek-bones, and, in addition, the spine, thigh-bones, hoofs etc. The animal body serves pure natural purposes and acquires by this dependence on the merely material aspect of nourishment an expression of spiritual absence. (Hegel 1998: 729)

In case of the human, the mouth and other organs which were the most important for the animal with its practical relation to things go on the background, since human relation is theoretical.

Therefore the human face has a second centre in which the soulful and spiritual relation to things is manifested. This is in the upper part of the face, in the intellectual brow and, lying under it, the eye, expressive of the soul, and what surrounds it.... Through this emphasis on the forehead, while the mouth and cheek-bones are secondary, the human face acquires a spiritual character. (ibid.)

It is interesting to compare this speculation with that of Bataille, who, among others, shared with Hegel such a perception of the animal body as dominated by the mouth. As he writes in 1930 in his short essay 'Mouth',

The mouth is the beginning or, if one prefers, the prow of animals; in the most characteristic cases, it is the most living part, in other words, the most terrifying for neighbouring animals. But man does not have a simple architecture like beasts, and it is not even possible to say where he begins … it is the eyes or the forehead that play the meaningful role of an animal's jaws. (Bataille 1985: 59)

However, Bataille, in his peculiar manner, supplements this observation with an anxiety, or maybe a fascination, produced by the animal nature of man, by saying that in moments of excitement, anger and so on, an open mouth reveals our obscene, 'explosive' physical impulses. Whence, he concludes, 'the narrow constipation of a strictly human attitude, the magisterial look of the face with a *closed mouth*,[3] [is] as beautiful as a safe' (60).

For Hegel, what is really and truly beautiful is a Greek profile as an artistic model, which ideally combines the individual and the universal, and in which animal traces are almost erased, even in the mouth, for the spirit's good.

By softening and smoothing the lines, the Greek profile introduces a beautiful harmony into the gentle and unbroken connection between the forehead and the nose and so between the upper and lower parts of the face. The effect of this connection is that the nose is made more akin to the forehead and therefore, by being drawn up towards the spiritual part, acquires itself a spiritual expression and character. Smelling becomes as it were theoretical, smelling becomes a keen nose for the spiritual ….

Something similar is true of the mouth too. It does have the purpose of being a tool for satisfying hunger and thirst, but it does also express spiritual states, moods, and passions. Even in animals it serves in this respect for ejaculations, but in man for speech, laughter, sighing, etc., and in this way the lines of the mouth already have a characteristic connection with the eloquent communication of spiritual states or of joy, grief, etc. (Hegel 1998: 730)

Hegel continues his analysis of the sculptural expression of the face formation by referring to the fact that 'the Chinese, Jews, and Egyptians regarded other, indeed opposite, formations as just as beautiful or more so', and then argues against the conclusion that therefore 'there is no proof that the Greek profile is the model of genuine beauty', or that there is no absolute model of the perfect beauty. Such a kind of conclusion, for him, is 'only superficial chatter'.

The Greek profile is not to be regarded as an external and fortuitous form; it belongs to the ideal of beauty in its own independent nature because (i) it is that facial formation in which the expression of the spirit puts the merely natural wholly into the background, and (ii) it is the one which most escapes fortuitousness of form without exhibiting mere regularity and banning every sort of individuality. (ibid.)

Of course, such statement cannot but attract the attention of contemporary critics. Thus, Elisabeth de Fontenay draws our attention to a necessary connection, which rises from here, between speciesism and racism.

For Hegel deduced from a comparative analysis of features – similarities or differences between human beings and animals, on the one hand, and human beings among themselves, on the other – an objective reality, where the levels of spirituality manifest themselves …. If one wanted to mock him, like Molière did with Aristotle, one could say that certain humans, certain human races, more than others, have their spirit down in matter, and visibly approximate the animal species. (Fontenay 1998: 539)

In his turn, Andrew Benjamin, who investigates the figures of the animal and the Jew in their relation to the problem of the 'other' in Hegel, emphasizes that the 'other' here appears as a particularity (or a disease) that is to be historically overcome by the universal humanity.

The sculpture of others – 'the Chinese, Jews and Egyptians' – is distanced from the ideal of beauty and thus from the connection that sculpture may have had to the spiritual. The history of sculpture in its development can, in the end, do without animals, and can have surpassed works that are not the expression of the spiritual. Their presence is limited to a moment within history, a moment whose presence is there to be overcome. (Benjamin 2007a: 76)

The gesture of overcoming is, indeed, absolutely crucial in Hegel's dialectics. There is no single moment in the unfolding of history which could be described as a pure positivity. No, the way of spirit consists of a series of difficult steps of self-negating and self-overcoming, including the 'animal' self. This negative move can be represented, in particular, by the human being's upright posture, which is, in Hegel, a result of a conscious and spontaneous act. Upright posture is another criterion involved in drawing a line between human and animal bodies. On the one hand, it is closely related to the function of the mouth, which in the human being loses its priority also because this being literally rears its head – whereas in animals mouth and spine are on the same line. On the other hand, for Hegel it indicates the free will, without which animals *cannot even stay erect.*

> The first point which offers itself for even superficial consideration about *position* is man's upright posture. The animal body runs parallel with the ground, jaws and eye pursue the same direction as the spine, and the animal cannot of itself independently annul this relation of itself to gravity. The opposite is the case with man, because the eye, looking straight outwards, has its natural directions always at right angles to the line of gravity and the body. Like the animals, man can go on all fours and little children do so in fact; but as soon as consciousness begins to awaken, man tears himself loose from being tied to the ground like an animal, and stands erect by himself. This standing is an act of will, for, if we give up willing to stand, our body collapses and falls to the ground. For this very reason the erect position has in it an expression of the spirit, because this rising from the ground is always connected with will and therefore with the spirit and its inner life. (Hegel 1998: 739)

Of course, free will is needed not just to stay erect. It is needed – and for Elisabeth de Fontenay, this is a dramatic crossing point between Hegel's *Naturphilosophie* and his *Rechtsphilosophie* – to possess and to manage one's life. What is involved here, in humans, is their awareness of death, which introduces an act of free will as a basic principle of human life. It is not that animals do not feel and suffer, as in Descartes. It is just the opposite: they do feel and suffer a lot, but they are unaware of death, they cannot truly die and death does not exist for them as a matter of consciousness and concern. Since animals do not really own their death, they cannot really possess their life, and an animal cannot therefore be the subject of law – as Hegel states in his *Philosophy of Right* (Fontenay 1998: 542). Animals cannot possess their life and death, but *we* can possess not only ours but also theirs. As de Fontenay concludes, this is how the metaphysical machinery operates: it gives humans all the power to dispose of animal life in their own way, according to their own needs and desires. De Fontenay's aim is thus to have done with this 'bloody tautology' (543).

It is difficult not to agree with this just demand, which emerges from the desire to rehabilitate animals after long centuries of repression, in every sense of the word. In solidarity with this critical discourse, we should, however, remind ourselves that it draws its legitimacy from the twentieth-century ethico-political emancipatory agenda and the general theoretical intention – from Heidegger and Bataille, through poststructuralism and deconstruction, to contemporary post-humanism – to do away with the entire metaphysical tradition, to go beyond it. However, I cannot but absolutely agree with Lacan, who summed up this intention already in 1955: 'I don't much like hearing that we have *gone beyond* Hegel, the way one hears we have *gone beyond* Descartes. We go beyond everything and always end up in the same place' (Lacan 1991b: 71).

If we want to catch at least part of the cat that jumped out of the metaphysical bag, we should go back to the point beyond which we claim to have gone (according to Lacan, we are still there) and look for another Hegel. Although this other will actually be the same Hegel, the Hegel of the totality of the Great system, in this system animals will play a more ambiguous and at the same time a more important role.[4]

We should go back to the before of the beyond, because, according to the aforementioned tendency to focus exclusively on the repressive aspect of the human-animal distinction, we can very quickly end up with a purely ethical concern. Such a concern does not lead us far enough, since it remains stuck at the surface of the all-too-human self-consciousness or, better, the bad conscience of philosophy, where all animal traces have already been erased. Therefore, we can go back to the point that Elisabeth de Fontenay briefly evokes as the first (phenomenological) tendency of Hegel and then hurriedly leaves it behind, as if it were something less significant. In order to do that, we need only go back to the passage from the radical Cartesian *exclusion* to the radical Hegelian *inclusion*, where the animal first appears as *subjectivity*.

During the Classical Age, the place of madness was, as Foucault puts it, 'in a zone of exclusion, from which it will only escape in part in Hegel's *Phenomenology of Spirit*' (Foucault 2006: 46). Together with a madman, particularly in the second volume of the *Encyclopaedia of the Philosophical Sciences*, an animal, this insane creature, will come out of the night and into the light of reason. If both social and intellectual practices of exclusion and isolation, described by Foucault, were functioning as a kind of 'hygienic' measure, aiming to prevent the spread of insanity, animality, poverty, idleness and other phenomena which threatened the frail domain of classical reason and the hierarchical order it established, then at a certain moment, this order becomes strong enough to fearlessly include and welcome again the hitherto rejected elements. Or, better – and this is already something else – after exploring all of the resources of the police, it discovers these elements within itself and gets ready to face them and to accept them as constitutive moments.

The police do not work effectively any more, because the 'enemy', the 'other' of reason, cannot easily be sent away, excluded or confined. Because 'I, myself' am 'potentially mad', or, as Lacan would repeat after Rimbaud, 'I is an other' (*'Je est un autre'*, Lacan 1991b, 2: 7). Thus, according to Žižek,

> As Hegel puts it in proto-Foucauldian terms, madness is not an accidental lapse, distortion, 'illness' of human spirit, but something which is inscribed into an individual spirit's basic ontological constitution, for to be human means to be potentially mad [...] Although not a factual necessity, madness is a formal possibility constitutive of human mind: it is something whose threat has to be overcome if we are to emerge as 'normal' subjects, which means that 'normality' can only arise as the overcoming of this threat. (Žižek 2012: 349)

In Hegel's philosophical system, reason is invested with such force and will that it declares its ability to capture and absorb the entire hostile sphere of the negativity of experience, including the experience of animality, of madness and even of death. The end of universal humanity – the end in both senses, as finalization and achievement of its principal task – is to provide matter with a realization of its proper spiritual content, to make it truly reasonable through the unfolding of the system of science. Any substance should thus be an opportunity for the subject – in a negative movement, which is at the same time a totality of spirit, having to pass through alienation and rupture, and to face finitude in order to overcome it. And finitude has to be comprehended through nature, which is 'the Idea in the guise of externality' (Hegel 2007: 418). Nature is a mirror of spirit, its negation, its objective, external, alienated existence, its existence in the form of otherness. In this mirror, spirit should recognize itself in order to acquire itself in its unity. The last sentence of this volume runs as follows:

> The aim of these lectures has been to give a picture of Nature in order to subdue this Proteus: to find in this externality only the mirror of ourselves, to see in Nature a free reflex of spirit: to know God, not in the contemplation of him as spirit, but in this his immediate existence. (445)

Hegel's philosophy of nature passes through all the levels and forms of inorganic and organic matter. Geological nature, crystals, oceans and atmosphere – everything seems alive and filled with sounds, light and the many and various shapes of existence. No one, nothing, not even the smallest mushroom or the trifling jellyfish, could hide from the eye of Hegel's omniscience. The philosopher is literally obsessed with the desire to include everything and everybody in the system of spirit and to make every point of the universe participate in the process of becoming. As if we were witnessing the most thorough stocktaking or inventory of nature, which aimed to appropriate all its wealth. Nothing should get lost or, worse still, be excluded; everything and everybody are welcome in the menagerie of spirit. The unity or even the solitude of spirit is reflected in the abundant multiplicity of nature. Animals, too, are now becoming a very important element of totality and have therefore to be thoroughly classified.

In the meantime, human culture has various modes of classifying animals. One can find a number of totally different attempts and approaches in myth, religion, science and the arts, sometimes as ridiculous as, for example, that of J.L. Borges' Chinese encyclopaedia as quoted by Foucault:

> … animals are divided into: (a) belonging to the emperor, (b) embalmed, (c) tame, (d) sucking pigs, (e) sirens, (f) fabulous, (g) stray dogs, (h) included in the present classification, (i) frenzied, (j) innumerable, (k) drawn with a very fine camelhair brush, (1) *et cetera*, (m) having just broken the water pitcher, (n) that from a long way off look like flies. (Foucault 1973: xv)

Foucault begins the *Order of Things* with the declaration that this classification produced in him a 'laughter that shattered all the familiar landmarks' of his thought ('of my thought – of *our* thought' (ibid.)). According to Foucault, what makes us laugh here is, roughly speaking, a heterogeneity or heterotopia, the absence of a unifying principle, which is really unthinkable in the Western tradition, with its 'age-old distinction between the Same and the Other' (ibid.). What is astonishing here is not, Foucault says, 'simply the oddity of unusual juxtapositions' but 'the fact that the common ground on which such meetings are possible has itself been destroyed'; 'what is impossible is not the propinquity of the things listed, but the very site on which their propinquity would be possible' (ibid., xvi). Since for Hegel, 'there is only one animal type, and all the varieties are merely modifications of it' (Hegel 2007: 418), it could look like his classification of animals is precisely the opposite of the 'Chinese' taxonomy in Borges. However, this is not quite true.

For Hegel, classification itself is a big problem, and this problem consists namely in the gap between external reality, or nature, and notion. As he says,

> In studying the classification of animals, the method followed is to search for a common feature to which the concrete forms [*Gebilde*] can be reduced, that is, to a simple, sensuous determinateness which therefore, is also an external one. But there are no such simple determinations. (417)

Hegel is thus aware of the fact that 'the variety and profusion of living forms does not admit of any general feature' (ibid.), or, as Foucault puts it, that there is no 'common ground'. There is no common ground in reality or nature itself, but, according to Hegel, one should search for it in another domain, which in no way coincides with nature, that is, on the side of spirit and science. While Aristotle, a naturalist, for instance, begins from empirical reality in order to adjust his theory to this reality as much as possible, Hegel insists that we have to begin with theory, with the concept, with 'general determinations'. And here we find the famous formula: if reality does not fit the notion, then it is reality's problem, not the notion's.

> On the contrary, therefore, it is general determinations which must be made the rule and natural forms compared with it. If they do not tally with it but exhibit certain correspondences, if they agree with it in one respect but not in another, then it is not the rule, the characteristic of the genus and class, etc., which is to be altered, as if this had to conform to these existences, but, conversely, it is the latter which ought to conform to the rule; and in so far as this actual existence does not do so, the defect belongs to *it*. (ibid.)

The domain of the concept is thus not one that should correspond to a certain reality of nature or reflect it, but rather one that subordinates this reality with all its particularities, to the universal. As Mladen Dolar notes,

> For Hegel facts cannot contradict theory not because of their lowly nature, but because they can only be facts if they are seized by the concept, a fact can acquire the dignity of a fact only by virtue of a theory which has selected it and presented it as relevant. (Dolar 2012)

In the meantime, let us notice that the universality of the concept requires a specific philosophical attitude, a kind of primordial *faith in the notion*. Hegel establishes a certain ethos of truth, according to which if there is something wrong with reality, in the sense that it does not fit the notion, does not conform to its classifications and general determinations and therefore cannot be explained by it, it is not because the reality is simply inadequate to the notion but because it lags behind it; and if this is so, then one should believe that, after all, the notion would not let one down and that reality ought to raise itself to its level.

> One must start from the Notion; and even if, perhaps, the Notion cannot yet give an adequate account of the 'abundant variety' of Nature so-called, we must nevertheless have faith in the Notion though many details are as yet unexplained. ... The Notion, however, is valid in its own right; the particulars then will soon find their explanation. (Hegel 2007: 358–359)

In other words, nature is not an osseous and unchangeable given, but a reality which transforms itself according to the logic of truth, introduced by the spirit unfolding itself in history.

To restrict oneself to referring this ethos of the philosopher solely to his idealism is to go awry. Of course, Hegel himself explicitly characterizes his position as idealism, 'which recognises the Idea through the whole of Nature', and which is 'at the same time realism' (358). However, if we want to get things right, we should be careful to understand just how radical this statement is, for from here, there is only one tiny, but very significant, decisive and indeed voluntarist step to what is taken up in Marx's eleventh thesis on Feuerbach: 'philosophers have only interpreted the world, in various ways; the point is to change it'.

With Hegel, theory, tired of trying to catch reality by the tail, declares its own pre-eminence. Contradiction was no longer indicated a problem in a theory which did not correspond to reality, but a problem in empirical reality which did not correspond to its notion. Nevertheless, the lack of any desire to narrow the gulf between theory and reality does not give us any indication as to whether the rule of general determinations is true or false, but rather demonstrates that reality, as it is, has serious flaws and presents a problem, and as true as notions might be, these deficiencies keep history and life from moving on far enough to catch up with their notions, as Hegel would have wanted. Our reality, the one we deal with every day, is neither an illusion nor the truth. This reality is real, but it is no less false, and thus theory should at once abandon its autonomy and become practice in order to make it true (this would be already a Marxian step).

One of the major points could be that, before any proletarian, the figure of the animal brings us to this passage, but in order to get to this point, we should first make a preliminary investigation of the vulnerable point at which, rather than the notion failing to follow nature, nature fails to follow the notion. If nature is the mirror of spirit, then this mirror is distorting,[5] but looking at oneself in this mirror is something that nevertheless makes sense, because it is precisely from these distortions and dramatic non-coincidences that historical subjectivity emerges.

Such a preliminary investigation passes through the Hegelian classification of animals, which proceeds from the so-called most primitive to the most developed, from worms to humans. Hegel bases his classification on the tradition beginning with Aristotle, and then developed by Cuvier and Lamarck. First of all, Aristotle divides living beings into animals that have blood and animals that do not. All the animals with blood, according to Aristotle, have a spine. Later on, this principle was refuted, but its essence remained in place as a kind of basis for further scientific constructions. Thus, in Lamarck, animals are divided into vertebrates and invertebrates. George Cuvier combined the principles of both Lamarck and Aristotle: in his theory, vertebrates have red blood, and invertebrates have white. Generally speaking, Lamarck thinks the same way, but he defines blood through the intensity of its red colour. Therefore, according to him, invertebrates do not have true blood, which is red, and so on. However, according to all these classifications, invertebrates and the bloodless still belong to the same fauna as vertebrates with blood (422). The presence or absence of the blood or the bones allows one to put an infinite variety of living beings into a certain order, and, of course, we should not forget that this order is traditionally a hierarchical one: thus, invertebrates without blood are at the bottom, whereas vertebrates with blood are at the top.

In general, Hegel accepts the traditional division of animals into invertebrates ('worms, molluscs, shell-fish etc.' (423)) and vertebrates. The further classification of vertebrates is based 'more simply on the Elements of their inorganic nature: earth, air, and water' (424), to which their bodies are adapted according to their notion. And thus we have land animals, birds and fish:

'The true land animals, the mammals, are the most perfect; then come birds, and the least perfect are fish' (425).

I would like to draw attention to one detail, which seems marginal, but which is in fact very important. In the further descriptions of mammals, we find a brief note on 'reptiles and amphibians', which are 'intermediate forms which belong partly to land and partly to water', and this is why, for Hegel, 'there is something repulsive about them' (ibid.). The question would be the following: Why, in fact, does he not like them? On a close reading, it turns out that Hegel's repulsion towards reptiles accompanies his crucial theoretical attitude.

As is well known, intermediate forms are usually taken as a proof of the idea of evolution. However, for Hegel, there is and can be no evolution or generation in nature.

It has been an inept conception of ancient and also recent Philosophy of Nature to regard the progression and transition of one natural form and sphere into a higher as an outwardly-actual production which, however, to be made clearer, is relegated to the *obscurity* of the past. It is precisely externality which is characteristic of Nature, that is, differences are allowed to fall apart and to appear as indifferent to each other: the dialectical Notion which leads forward the *stages*, is the inner side of them. A thinking consideration must reject such nebulous, at bottom, sensuous ideas, as in particular the so-called *origination*, for example, of plants and animals from water, and then the *origination* of the more highly developed animal organisms from the lower, and so on. (20)

This is a point on which Hegel has been much criticized, by Benedetto Croce, for example, according to whom,

> The evolution and the dialectic of the concepts, in Hegel's philosophy of nature, is purely ideal. It leaves natural species intact, and indeed proclaims their fixity. ... This is sheer hostility to the hypothesis of transformation and it is what might be expected from Hegel, who does not recognize any historicity in nature. (Croce 1969: 164–165)

Indeed, Hegel's negative attitude towards the idea of evolution derives precisely from his aforementioned radical idealism. The existence of the so-called intermediate forms, for Hegel, demonstrates not the evolutionary process of transformation, but just the 'impotence of Nature to remain true to the Notion and to adhere to thought-determinations in their purity' (Hegel 2007: 423). It is thus not by chance that he clearly prefers 'the true animals' and has no special sympathy for whales, reptiles, amphibians and so on. The Hegelian amphibian is a mistake of nature, a defective individual, which did not succeed in following the idea, got stuck in between the air and the earth and therefore 'presents a sorry picture'.

> But the fact that in the Cetacea, the land animal falls back again into the water; that in the amphibians and reptiles the fish again climbs on to the land, where it presents a sorry picture, snakes, for example, possessing the rudiments of feet which serve no purpose; that the bird becomes an aquatic bird and in the duck-billed platypus (*ornithorhynchus*) even crosses over to the class

of land animals, and in the stork becomes a camel-like animal that is covered more with hair than with feathers; that the land animal and the fish attained to flight, the former in vampires and bats, and the latter in the flying fish: all this does not efface the fundamental difference, which is not a common, a shared difference, but a difference in and for itself. The great distinctions must be adhered to in face of these imperfect products of Nature, which are only mixtures of such determinations. (425)

Here lies one of the central principles of the *Philosophy of Nature*, which shows clearly how the Hegelian system works – only as a totality of truth:

Animal nature is the truth of vegetable nature, vegetable of mineral; the earth is the truth of the solar system. In a system, it is the most abstract term which is the first, and the truth of each sphere is the last; but this again is only the first of a higher sphere. It is the necessity of the Idea which causes each sphere to complete itself by passing into another higher one, and the variety of forms must be considered as necessary and determinate. (21)

The dialectics of spirit thus consists in the inner unity of truth; the becoming is not a visible process of transformation: 'The land animal did not develop naturally out of the aquatic animal, nor did it fly into the air on leaving the water, not did perhaps the bird fall back to earth' (ibid.).

In the case of nature with its variety and multiplicity, one becomes 'other' in itself, and the spirit externalizes itself only through the individualization of beings in their singularity, not in their mixing. Nature, the distorted mirror of the unity of spirit, is the domain of difference. This is how it manifests itself as substance becoming subject, given that the subject is not only that which transforms itself but also that which always remains the same through these transformations. The inner dialectic of becoming expresses itself in a given individual shape, whether it be a stone, a flower, a mineral, a tree, a horse or a woman. And all this can exist only in totality, the one being a truth of the other and coming to relate to it.

After all, one can say that, in a way, Hegel's encyclopaedia of animals does not differ that much in this respect from Borges' 'Chinese' one, where we can find both of the two kinds of animals: those 'included in the present classification' on the one hand, and '*et cetera*' on the other. *Et cetera*, thus, are also *included* like those Hegelian bats and vampires which do not fit the notion well enough but still exist in this abundance of animal life, if only as mistakes of nature (given that a mistake, in Hegel, is also a part of a process of truth.

Furthermore, Hegel proceeds with his classification of mammals by defining them according to their behaviour 'as individuals towards other animals', or according to the parts or tools with which animals come to relate to each other.

By opposing itself as an individual to its non-organic nature through its weapons, the animal demonstrates that it is a subject for itself. On this basis, the classes of mammals are very accurately distinguished: αα. into animals whose feet are hands – man and the monkey (the monkey is a satire on man, a satire which it must amuse him to see if he does not take himself too seriously but is willing to laugh at himself); ββ. into animals whose extremities are claws – *dogs*, wild beasts like the *lion*, the king of beasts; γγ. into *rodents* in which the teeth are especially shaped; δδ. into *cheiroptera*, which have a membrane stretched between the toes, as occurs even in some rodents (these animals come nearer to dogs and monkeys); εε. into sloths, in which some of the toes are missing altogether and have become claws; ζζ. into animals with *fin-like* limbs, the Cetacea; ηη. into hoofed animals, like *swine, elephants* (which have a trunk), horned cattle, horses etc. (427)

Of course, among mammals and, generally speaking, among animals, man is most perfect – and the abovementioned monkey who also has hands 'is a satire on man'. In a way, it is not only that the monkey is the most anthropomorphous animal but also that all other animals in classical Western-European philosophy, since Aristotle, are a 'satire' or 'parody' of man (diametrically opposed to this tradition of mimesis is the Bataillean prehistory, where it is a man who imitates an animal and hides himself beneath an animal head, and where a figuration of man 'tends toward caricature').

It is not surprising that, in his speculations about animals, Hegel refers to Aristotle. Thus, the three types of organic life in Hegel – plant, animal and human – correspond to the three souls in Aristotle.

The animal also has the plant-nature, a relationship to light, air, and water: but in addition it has sensation, to which is also added in man, thought. Aristotle thus speaks of three souls, the vegetable, animal, and human, as the three determinations of the development of the Notion. (355)

In this respect, one should not forget that both the Aristotelian mimetic cosmos and the Hegelian totality exist due to inclusion and the fundamental unity of all elements, and if for Aristotle, as Simondon puts it, the principle of this unity is *life*, then for Hegel such a principle will be *subjectivity* and *negativity*. Again, substance is becoming subject.

Hegel describes all organisms as subjectivities, and animals are also on the list, between plants and humans. As Sebastian Rand says, 'What it is for an animal to be a subject is just for it to do this: to sense, in this way, itself in sensing another, and to make this self-sensation into sensation of an other by tying the sensory activity to other activities of differentiation and unification' (Rand 2010).

Animals are subjects in so far as they are negatively related to certain sensual objects, and if one wants a perfect example of negativity, one should go back to a wonderful passage in the *Phenomenology of Spirit*, where Hegel, criticizing sense-certainty, compares the animal with an initiate of the Eleusinian mysteries.

In this respect, what one can say to those who make assertions about the truth and reality of sensuous objects is that they should be sent back to the most elementary school of wisdom, namely, to the old Eleusinian mysteries of Ceres

and Bacchus and that they have yet to learn the mystery
of the eating of bread and the drinking of wine. This is so
because the person who has been initiated into these secrets
not merely comes to doubt the being of sensuous things.
Rather, he is brought to despair of them; in part he brings
about their nothingness, and in part he sees them do it to
themselves. Nor are the animals excluded from this wisdom.
To an even greater degree, they prove themselves to be the
most deeply initiated in such wisdom, for they do not stand
still in the face of sensuous things, as if those things existed
in themselves. Despairing of the reality of those things and in
the total certainty of the nullity of those things, they, without
any further ado, simply help themselves to them and devour
them. Just like the animals, all of nature celebrates these
revealed mysteries which teach the truth about sensuous
things. (Hegel 1979: 65)

In this sense, one might see in Hegelian Eleusinian animals
a kind of subversive parody of the Cartesian *cogito*, the latter
suspended between its own certainty and the armchair radicalism
of its doubt about the sensuous world. It is not that these animals
have some 'doubts' about the existence of sensuous objects; no,
as Hegel says, they are despairing (*Verzweiflung*) of them, and in
despair, they actively negate those objects. Their animality appears
as subjectivity through the negative gesture towards reality, by
which they acquire their freedom. All Hegelian subjectivities do
so, with the only necessary condition being that, from one level to
the next, their freedom becomes less individually restricted and

more general and universal. The levels of freedom are increasing. For example, while plants are still attached to their places, animals have already acquired freedom of movement, and even though they cannot stay erect, they start to overcome gravity and to freely determine their movements:

> The animal has freedom of self-movement because its subjectivity is, like light, ideally freed from gravity, a free time which, as removed from real externality, spontaneously determines its place. (Hegel 2007: 352)
>
> The particularization of place lies therefore in the animal's own power, and it is not posited by an other; it is the animal itself which gives itself its place. In any other thing, this particularization is fixed, because a thing is not a self which is for itself. True, the animal does not escape from the general determination of being in a particular place; but *this* place is posited by the animal itself. And it is for this very reason that the subjectivity of the animal is not simply distinguished from external Nature, but the animal distinguishes itself from it; and this is an extremely important distinction, this positing of itself as the pure negativity of *this* place, and *this* place, and so on. (354)

Moreover, Hegelian animals have a voice, this 'high privilege', which is 'the closest to Thought' (355). Therefore birds, as both freely flying and singing, evoke in Hegel a special perplexity. And if St. Francis' little birds, converted to Christianity, could by singing spread the Word of God, which they have heard from man, then the Hegelian bird already brings to the world its own message.

The animal makes manifest that it is inwardly for-itself, and this manifestation is voice. But it is only the sentient creature that can show outwardly that it is sentient. Birds of the air and other creatures emit cries when they feel pain, need, hunger, repletion, pleasure, joyfulness, or are in heat: the horse neighs when it goes to battle; insects hum; cats purr when pleased. But the voice of the bird when it launches forth in song is of a higher kind; and this must be reckoned as a special manifestation in birds over and above that of voice generally in animals. For while fish are dumb in their element of water, birds soar freely in theirs, the air; separated from the objective heaviness of the earth, they fill the air with themselves, and utter their self-feeling in their own particular element. Metals have sound, but this still is not voice; voice is the spiritualized mechanism which thus utters itself. The inorganic does not show its specific quality until it is stimulated from outside, gets struck; but the animal sounds of its own accord. What is subjective announces its psychic nature [*als dies Seelenhafte*] in vibrating inwardly and in merely causing the air to vibrate. (354)

However, the voice of the Hegelian animal is devoid of sense. The animal voice is not yet a language; it is not a meaningful sound. Being is manifested, but nothing is said. And only in man does spirit arrive at its proper expression in language. In Hegel, as Jean Hyppolite emphasizes,

It is language which creates the individuation of the Universal, or the manifestation of the existential unity of the Singular and the Universal. Language announces simultaneously the object of which one is speaking and the subject who speaks; language is the voice that 'the moment it speaks, recognizes itself as no longer a voice without a self'. (Hyppolite 1969: 177)

Mastering language is the privilege of man – this is one of the most unshakeable pillars of philosophy, and apparently Hegel is sitting on top of this pillar. But, as emphasized by Agamben, who, in his book *Language and Death*, follows Hegel very closely in this respect, it is precisely from the 'emptiness' of the animal voice that human language emerges. Agamben quotes the *Jenenser Realphilosophie*, where Hegel describes the process through which the voice acquires its meaning and becomes 'the voice of consciousness', that is the process of articulation and speech.

The empty voice of the animal acquires a meaning that is infinitely determinant in itself. The pure sound of the voice, the vowel, is differentiated since the organ of the voice presents its articulation with its differences. This pure sound is interrupted by mute [consonants], the true and proper arrestation of mere resonation. It is primarily through this that every sound has a meaning for itself, since the differences of mere sound in song are not determinate for themselves, but only in reference to the preceding and following sounds. Language, inasmuch as it is sonorous and articulated, is the voice of consciousness because of the fact that every sound has a meaning. (Agamben 1991: 44)[6]

Commenting on this passage, in which 'the articulation appears … as a process of differentiation, of interruption and preservation of the animal voice', Agamben raises the following questions:

> Why does this articulation of the animal voice transform it into the voice of consciousness, into memory and language? What was contained in the 'pure sound' of the 'empty' animal voice such that the simple articulation and preservation of this voice would give rise to human language as the voice of consciousness? (ibid.)

In the search for an answer, he refers to another Hegelian statement on the animal voice: 'Every animal finds a voice in its violent death; it expresses itself as a removed-self [*als aufgehobnes Selbst*]' (Hegel 1967: 161). If so, then, according to Agamben,

> We may now understand why the articulation of the animal voice gives life to human language and becomes the voice of consciousness. The voice, as expression and memory of the animal's death, is no longer a mere, natural sign that finds its other outside of itself. And although it is not yet meaningful speech, it already contains within itself the power of the negative and of memory. … In dying, the animal finds its voice, it exalts the soul in one voice, and, in this act, it expresses and preserves itself *as dead.* … Only because the animal voice is not truly 'empty' (in the passage from Hegel 'empty' simply means lacking in any determinate significance), but contains the death of the animal, can human language, articulating and arresting the pure sound of this voice (the vowel) – that is to say,

articulating and retaining the *voice of death* – become the *voice of consciousness*, meaningful language. (Agamben 1991: 45)

That is why 'the death of the animal is the becoming of consciousness' (Hegel 1967: 164). From here one may conclude, following Agamben's logic, that human consciousness and articulated language not only derive from the death of the animal but preserve and carry within them a kind of undead animal, which is itself already a memory. Human consciousness keeps in itself this animal that still remembers itself 'as removed'.[7] The animal pretends to be completely forgotten by this negative move, which Bataille will call *sacrifice*. Sacrifice is a moment which is implicated 'in the whole movement of the *Phenomenology* – where it is the negativity of death, insofar as it is assumed, which makes a man of the human animal', he writes in *Hegel, Death, and Sacrifice*.

> Concerning sacrifice, I can essentially say that, on the level of Hegel's philosophy, man has, in a sense, revealed and founded human truth by sacrificing; in sacrifice he destroyed the animal in himself, allowing himself and the animal to survive only as that non-corporeal truth which Hegel describes and which makes of man – in Heidegger's words – a being unto death (*Sein zum Tode*), or – in the words of Kojève himself – 'death which lives a human life'. (Bataille 1997: 286–288)

However, the animal 'which I am', this very human animality, which was thus negated by the universal spirit in order to give rise to consciousness, knowledge and history, is still there; it never completely disappears. In claiming this, Bataille refers to the brutal fact that if one literally destroys one's own animal life, if one destroys the animal life which was supposed to be the bearer of consciousness, the human will die together with the animal, at the very same moment. Therefore, for Bataille, what is essential in sacrifice is its fake, spectacular character.

> For when the animal being supporting him dies, the human being himself ceases to be. In order for man to reveal himself ultimately for himself, he would have to die, but he would have to do it while living – watching himself ceasing to be. In other words, death itself would have to become (self-) consciousness at the very moment that it annihilates the conscious being. In a sense, this is what takes place (what at least is on the point of taking place, or which takes place in a fugitive, ungraspable manner) by means of a subterfuge. In the sacrifice, the sacrificer identifies himself with the animal that is struck down dead. And so he dies in seeing himself die, and even, in a certain way, by his own will, one in spirit with the sacrificial weapon. But it is a comedy! (286–287)

To put it very simply, the sacrificial animal always replaces the human being; they always die 'for us'. Sacrifice is a feint: it is the other who will die; the death we overcome is not truly 'ours', but the one we witness (from here, there is a huge Bataillean controversy on the dialectic of master and slave, where both parties feign one another). One might say, however, that, on the contrary, the death we witness here *is* 'ours' in the sense that it 'belongs' to us as 'internalized' or grasped as a fact of consciousness. Thus, according to Jean Hyppolite, in his commentary on Hegel,

> The animal is unconscious of the infinite totality of life in its wholeness, whereas man becomes the for-itself of that totality and internalizes death. That is why the basic experience of human self-consciousness is inseparable from the fundamental experience of death. (Hyppolite 1969: 26)

The 'fundamental experience' of internalized death constitutes a territory where psychoanalysis meets sacrifice – the paradoxical territory of the memory of the forgotten, inhabited by animals. But this is not a Hegelian land. This obscure crossing point is absent in Hegel, since for him there is no unconscious. What is left behind (let us call it, very roughly, animality) is not 'repressed', but surpassed; it is always still there as negated, but it never 'returns'. However, as Mladen Dolar and Slavoj Žižek never cease to emphasize, there is something which brings Hegel quite close to Freud and Lacan, where he speaks of human consciousness as based on a capacity to create a subjective unity out of itself: before 'consciousness', on the organic level, this 'self' is already essentially *split*. Life is split in itself, and the subject emerges from this split, from the sickness of the animal as an organic being. As Hyppolite puts it,

> However, even at the animal level there is a moment which foreshadows consciousness, namely, in sickness. In sickness the organism is divided against itself internally. Life which becomes lodged in a particular being is in conflict with life

in general. This conflict between the moment of particularity in relation to universal life constitutes, as in a sick organism, the positivity and destiny of history. Hegel had studied this schism within man and human history in his early works. By perceiving in organic illness a prefiguration of the consciousness which is always internally divided within itself, and is an unhappy consciousness in so far as it is the consciousness of 'the positivity of life as the unhappiness of life', Hegel alters the meaning of his comparison. Human self-consciousness is able to triumph just where the organism fails. (182)

This sickness characterizes the initial vulnerability of the living individual. In brief, as already discussed in the context of Andrew Benjamin's work, the deficiency of Hegelian animals, which should be overcome in humans, is in their inability to freely create themselves as an internal unity in order to resist and counter external reality. The natural being of an animal, exposed to the contingencies of the environment and the dangers of life with its 'perpetual violence', brings it to a state of incessant 'alternation of health and disease' and makes it essentially 'insecure, anxious and unhappy' (Hegel 2007: 417).

This aspect is thoroughly discussed by Andrew Benjamin:

The impossibility of self-constitution within the animal – a positioning that locates the animal's singularity and defines it as continually 'sick' – is explicable in a number of different ways. The most significant in this context is an explanation in terms of Hegel's distinction between 'impulse' (*Instinkt*) and 'drive' (*Trieb*) on the one hand, and the 'will' on the other. The will is that which enables 'Man' to stand above impulses and drives. Moreover, it is the will that allows Man to be equated with the wholly 'undetermined' while the animal is always already determined. (Benjamin 2007a: 67)

What Hegelian animals definitely lack is thus this indeterminacy, or, again, a free will, an incomparable freedom which, after all, allows human beings not only to stay erect but to take risks, negating their animal life which still remains hostage to the necessity reigning in the natural kingdom. In the meantime, the beast is still attached to the environment and depends on external conditions of its natural existence. Moreover, as always happens in classical philosophy, a certain *anthropological machine* starts to operate here, rejecting the essential sickness of the animal kingdom and also certain types of human: 'Man fashions the self in more interior fashion, although in southern latitudes he, too, does not reach the stage where his self, his freedom is objectively guaranteed' (Hegel 2007: 306).[8]

Imagine a stray animal lost in a contemporary city. In order to survive, it must work out its spatial orientation and disposition in relation to the road traffic, to various urban and industrial objects and to human beings, among many other things. In comparison with this, the life of the domesticated animal, given over to a human being's responsibility, is, indeed, much safer. This brings us to the idea that a higher level of freedom gives one the power to govern all those who have not managed to create their own internal unity. The question that follows would be, however, if animals and 'southern people' are not free enough and therefore exposed to the dangers and violence 'of the environment of external contingency', then are *we* ourselves, 'human beings', really and truly free?

This question extends beyond the domain of the metaphysics of transcendence with its inherent logic of sacrifice, and interrogates contemporary biopolitics. Here I would refer to Agamben's critique of the Bataillean conception of sacrifice together with the idea of the 'unsacrificeable existence' (proposed by Jean-Luc Nancy (1991b)). According to Agamben, the 'sacred' status of human life, and of life in general, has completely lost its relevance, since all life is now 'exposed to violence' without any constraints.

> In modernity, the principle of the sacredness of life is thus completely emancipated from sacrificial ideology, and in our culture the meaning of the term 'sacred' continues the semantic history of *homo sacer* and not that of sacrifice (and this is why the demystifications of sacrificial ideology so common today remain insufficient, even though they are correct). What confronts us today is a life that as such is exposed to a violence without precedent precisely in the most profane and banal ways. (Agamben 1998: 115)

One could say, then, that in such a disposition every person becomes a kind of 'insecure' Hegelian animal. It is not because Agamben thinks that the human being has 'lost' its transcendent status but because the author shifts registers and applies another kind of optics, a kind of historical genealogy, which infiltrates invariances of the metaphysical order by identifying alterations in the juridical order. And if, following Agamben's logic, the animalization of man is not just a side-effect, but a necessary result of the operation of the anthropological machine, we may conclude that any metaphysical presupposition about human superiority over animals will ultimately reduce us to this pitiful state.

However – to return to Hegel and to take into account his notion of a subjectivity prior to any anthropogenesis – it is paradoxically this position of animals (together with 'southern people', 'Jews', slaves in Haiti etc.), which renders them vulnerable to the violence to be found in both nature and ('Western') humanity, that in the Hegelian system, after all, carves out a space for all of the 'subhuman' creatures, and in the end gives them a very specific kind of chance. Their very life, in its essentially split nature, its sickness and unhappiness, already contains the force of negativity within itself, which can express itself as an anxiety, or, as Hegel says in his *Science of Logic*, an unrest: 'the *unrest* of the something in its limit in which it is immanent, an unrest which is the contradiction which impels something out beyond itself' (Hegel 1969: 128).

It is not just the animal in its natural environment that knows and experiences this unrest, which Nancy describes as *the restlessness of the negative* (Nancy 2002) or *becoming,* but every *something.* Every something at every moment is pushed beyond itself in its desire not to be what it is, to leave the place it occupies. This is the desperate unrest of the animal or the slave, in their ability to negate the world around them and in their desire to experience greater freedom, or, as Deleuze and Guattari put it, to escape, to find a way out.

This brings us right back to Kafka's transformations, becomings, individuations, mutations and monstrosities. Let us pause for a moment here and ask Deleuze and Guattari whether it is really true that for Kafka animal freedom does not matter? Is the way out always enough, as in the case of the ape which became man in the search for an escape? Does this man, this former ape, really tell the truth when he claims that he was never seeking freedom, but only a way out? Or, rather – if we suppose that he must be speaking the truth, for animals do not lie – did he finally find what he was searching for (a way out), or did he acquire something else (freedom)? If a real escape means an escape when there is no escape (a breakthrough), then freedom is something else.

Nancy, in his reading of Hegel, defines freedom as 'availability for sense': 'What Hegel first gives to think is this: sense never being given nor readily available, it is a matter of making oneself available for it, and this availability is called freedom' (Nancy 2002: 7). Might the Kafkian Ape Man, reporting for an academy, be a mutation of the Aristotelian mimetic animal – he is making a breakthrough, he finds a way out and he acquires something else, that which allows him to describe his experience of becoming, to give a sense to what has happened to him; he makes himself available for that sense. The ape gets the freedom that he was not searching for, freedom as a matter of sense, his self-relation.

There is, however, another example of mutation in Kafka, that of the dog-philosopher who dedicates his life to what he calls a scientific investigation of himself, of his instincts, his body and mind. By risking his life as a natural being, he creates a kind of distance, which helps him to observe the world around him and to relate to his previous life. And, similarly to the Ape Man, he is trying to explain his becoming retrospectively; he gives a sense to what happened to him earlier, addressing his previous animal life in its precariousness and unhappiness.

How much my life has changed, and yet how unchanged it has remained at bottom! When I think back and recall the time when I was still a member of the canine community, sharing in all its preoccupations, a dog among dogs, I find on closer examination that from the very beginning I sensed some discrepancy, some little maladjustment, causing a slight feeling of discomfort which not even the most decorous public functions could eliminate; more, that sometimes, no, not sometimes, but very often, the mere look at some fellow dog of my own circle that I was fond of, the mere look of him, as if I had just caught it for the first time, would fill me with helpless embarrassment and fear, even with despair. I tried to quiet my apprehensions as best I could; friends, to whom I divulged them, helped me; more peaceful times came – times, it is true, in which these sudden surprises were not lacking, but in which they were accepted with more philosophy, fitted into my life with more philosophy, including a certain melancholy and lethargy, it may be, but nevertheless allowing me to carry on as a somewhat cold, reserved, shy, and calculating, but all things considered normal enough dog. How, indeed, without these breathing spells, how could I have reached the age that I enjoy at present; how could I have fought my way through the serenity with which I contemplate the terrors of youth and endure the terrors of age; how could I have come to the point where I am able to draw the consequences of my admittedly unhappy, or, to put it more moderately, not very happy disposition, and live almost entirely in accordance with them? (Kafka 1995: 278)

In the case of the dog and in the case of the ape, both telling us their stories, an animal voice makes use of language, thanks to the self-relation of the present which retrospectively gives sense to the past. But there are, let's say, two different kinds of mimesis operating here: whereas the ape imitates what he thinks *is* (a free man), the dog imitates – and invents – what *has never been* – a new science. If the ape, even in his self-reflection, is still an object of observation on the part of existing human science, then the dog is the 'subject' in every sense of the word, 'the founding dog of a new science' (Dolar 2006: 187). A new science, which he practises as *freedom*. And besides, what makes this science so unique and so ultimate, what endows it with freedom, is precisely the dog's initial incapacity for it, his inadequacy, the limits he observes, in brief, his *animality*. It is not merely a constitutive moment of the new science but a necessary starting point for the breakthrough, without which freedom would never be possible.

The reason for that can be found in my incapacity for scientific investigation, my limited powers of thought, my bad memory, but above all in my inability to keep my scientific aim continuously before my eyes. All this I frankly admit, even with a certain degree of pleasure. For the more profound cause of my scientific incapacity seems to me to be an instinct, and indeed by no means a bad one … It was this instinct that made me – and perhaps for the sake of science itself – but a different science from that of today, an ultimate science – prize freedom higher than everything else. Freedom! Certainly such freedom as is possible today is a wretched business. But nevertheless freedom, nevertheless a possession. (Kafka 1995: 315–316)

In contrast to Deleuze and Guattari, who privilege the notion of escape over that of freedom, Mladen Dolar, commenting on the *Investigations of a Dog*, suggests that freedom is in fact Kafka's 'secret word'.

This is the last sentence of the story. The last word of it all, *le fin mot* as *le mot de fin*, is freedom, with an exclamation mark. Are we not victims of a delusion, should we not pinch ourselves, is it possible that Kafka actually utters this word? This may well be the only place where Kafka talks about freedom in explicit terms, but this does not mean that there is unfreedom everywhere else in his universe. Quite the opposite: freedom is there at all times, everywhere, it is Kafka's *fin mot*, like the secret word we dare not utter although it is constantly on our mind. … And there is the slogan, the program of a new science which would be able to treat it, to take it as its object, to pursue it, the ultimate science, the science of freedom. (Dolar 2006: 188)

What would this science be like? According to Dolar, 'Kafka lacks the proper word for it, he cannot name it – this is 1922 – but he had only to look around, to examine the ranks of his Jewish Austrian compatriots. Of course – psychoanalysis' (ibid.). Does this mean that the ultimate science would be the one that entails lying on a couch and telling stories? In a way, this may be the case, but I should add that as far as the dog is concerned, Hegel would be as important as Freud. The dog of the ultimate science is both a Freudian and a Hegelian dog. It is the animal that makes itself available for sense. This dog inaugurates a new science that allows him to say that *he was a dog*. It is the animal of retrospection which proclaims 'More philosophy!' Actually, it is a monster, an owl-dog, the owl being the Hegelian animal *par excellence*, the animal of retrospection: 'When philosophy paints its grey on grey, then has a form of life grown old, and with grey on grey it cannot be rejuvenated, but only known; the Owl of Minerva first takes flight with twilight closing in' (Hegel 1967: 13).

The properly philosophical animal appears afterwards and creates – that is, gives meaning to – what was beforehand. The owl creates the entire ensemble of creatures which were left behind, all those unhappy subjectivities, rampant throughout the Hegelian universe. And *vice versa*: the freedom of this ultimate, retrospective, philosophical or psychoanalytical animal needs to be anticipated beforehand, within animality itself, the bearer of subjectivity of this particular subject. We move from a retrospective to a prospective. Here, both the 'organic repression' of Freud's *Civilization and Its Discontents* and the

Hegelian sublation of animal nature meet an insoluble paradox. As emphasized by Cary Wolfe,

> The human being who only becomes human through an act of 'organic repression' has to *already* know, before it is human, that the organic needs to be repressed, and so the Freudian 'human' is caught in a chain of infinite supplementarity, as Derrida would put it, which can never come to rest at an origin that would constitute a break with animality. (Wolfe 1999: 118)

5

Unemployed animality

How has it come about that negativity is now associated exclusively with man in his creative activity? Why was subjectivity in its unrest attributed to humans alone, and why was dialectics, especially in the French thought of the twentieth century, associated with the metaphysical circle of man, being and language, from which animals and other non-human beings were excluded? One important step was the anthropologizing of negativity, a step taken by Alexander Kojève in his influential but debatable interpretation of Hegel, whom he read particularly through the lens of Heidegger's thought.

As is well known, Alexander Kojève, a nephew of Vasily Kandinsky, fled from revolutionary Russia and, after teaching philosophy in Paris for many years, later became a counsellor for economic and trade diplomacy and one of the creators of the European Union. From 1933 to 1939, he lectured on Hegel's *Phenomenology of Spirit* at the *École Pratique des Hautes Études*.

In the course of this seminar, Kojève read certain chapters of the German text, translated them into French and commented on them. Kojève's interpretation enjoyed the full confidence of his audience. He had a great talent as a narrator. In his interpretation, *Phenomenology of Spirit* is like a huge philosophical novel, with vividly drawn characters and memorable dramatic episodes.

One might summarize the crucial parts of Kojève's reading as follows: the beginning of time coincides with the appearance of man. Before this moment, there is no time. There is only natural being, or space, which is eternal and immutable. There are animals that inhabit this space. History begins when, at a certain point, *one of these animals turns into a man*. 'The real presence of Time in the World, therefore, is called Man. Time is Man, and Man is Time', says Kojève (Kojève 1969: 138). The appearance of man as an active, suffering, fighting and working nothingness will introduce history and time in by means of the process of the negation of natural being for the benefit of man's supernatural ideal goals:

Man must be an emptiness, a nothingness, which is not a pure nothingness, but something that is to the extent that it annihilates Being, in order to realize itself at the expense of Being and to nihilate in being. Man is negating Action, which transforms given Being and, by transforming it, transforms itself. (38)

Kojevian negativity has, therefore, a human face. He turns Hegelian ontology into anthropology. The condition of the appearance of man is his biological reality as a being capable of desire. Even if Kojève acknowledges that all living beings have the ability to desire, he thinks that man is the only one for whom this capacity is absolutely fundamental. Desire pushes man to act, and this action negates the object of desire, transforming and assimilating it, and thus creates some subjective reality. The desire of man as opposed to the desire of the animal is not a desire for this or that object.

> To be sure, the animal, too, has desires, and it acts in terms of these desires, by negating the real: it eats and drinks, just like man. But the animal's desires are natural; they are directed toward what is, and hence they are determined by what is. (138)

Here is the difference: the desire of the Kojèvian animal is related to the present; it desires something that *is*, that can be grasped immediately, whereas human desires are related to the future, to *what is not yet*: human beings desire the non-existent, supernatural phantasmatic objects. Moreover, in human beings the desire itself becomes an object of desire. Human beings want to be desired by other human beings, to be recognized by others in their human dignity; they are fighting for recognition, or, as Georges Bataille would have it, for *prestige*. This is how people open up history, which in turn becomes the history of struggles, wars and revolutions. That's how humans actively change the world according to their desires.

This brief description would need elaborating at great length, but the principle, which is very important for Kojève, is that the point of the end of history should coincide with the point of the beginning. This means that, at the end of history, *a human being should turn into an animal again*. This point is very ambiguous and at the same time it is crucial. Kojèvian history makes its round only once, with no repetition, and this is the history of becoming human, which (as Kojeve thinks) has already come to an end. To finish history, humanity has to create a universal homogeneous state of mutual recognition,[1] a state of the total gratification of all desires, and this actually occurs.

Following Kojève's logic, theoretically, this point has already been achieved. There is nothing left for humanity to do but to find the right state, some fitting social reality which would be a model for the further post-historical unfolding of the same. Nothing really new will ever happen again. In so far as such a totality is achieved, historical time, with its projections for the future, is over, and from now on we shall have to do only with the eternal present where all projects are realized and all desires are satisfied. At the end of history, man no longer needs to change the world, work and fight; satisfaction is obtainable here and now. Kojève claimed that, for Hegel, an embodiment of absolute spirit as a final historical point was the Napoleonic Empire: Hegel even called Napoleon the World Spirit, or the World Soul, after seeing the emperor in Jena riding a white horse.

There is nothing catastrophic in the apocalypses of Kojève[2]; the end does not look like a sudden tragic interruption of ongoing historical processes or people's lives. Rather, it is an achievement, an expected completion and a successful realization of a specific programme. Perhaps the task of Kojèvian history is to turn the unhappy animal into a happy one, and the human being, or history, time, and negativity, are nothing but the long way between the two.

However, after all, there is one question here that makes the whole story very interesting in its fallacy: what – or who – remains when history has come to an end? On the one hand, history means the development of spirit, self-consciousness and knowledge. Post-historical man is therefore a Wise Man who assimilates the consciousness of history and accomplishes history by means of self-consciousness. On the other hand, this post-historical Wise Man does not work, does not fight and does not desire in a human way anymore. He just gets immediate satisfaction, enjoying whatever makes him happy – arts, love, play, sport and so on. The Wise Man turns out to be an animal, but a very special type of animal – an animal who succeeds, in the course of the bloody history of struggles and revolutions, finally in appropriating all the wealth in the world, and who now has it all at his disposal. But, after all, is he an animal or a human being?

In 1948, Kojève acknowledged that if at the end of history man becomes an animal again, then this end is already here and now. He explains in his notes to the second edition of the *Introduction to the Reading of Hegel*:

At the period when I wrote the above note (1946), Man's return to animality did not appear unthinkable to me as a prospect for the future (more or less near). But shortly afterwards (1948) I understood that the Hegelian-Marxist end of History *was not yet to come, but was already a present here and now*, observing what was taking place around me and reflecting on what had taken place in the world since the Battle of Jena, I understood that Hegel was right to see in this battle the end of History properly so-called. In the end by this battle the vanguard of humanity virtually attained the limit and the aim, that is, the end, of Man's historical evolution. What has happened since then was but an extension in space of the universal revolutionary force actualized in France by Robespierre-Napoleon. From the authentically historical point of view, the two world wars with their retinue of large and small revolutions had only the effect of *bringing the backward civilizations of the peripheral provinces into line with the most advanced* (real or virtual) *European historical positions.* (160)

At around the time he composed this note, Kojève abandoned his philosophical career and became involved in state administration. He started to work for the French Ministry of Economic Affairs and became one of the chief planners of the European Common Market and one of the architects of the European Union. This choice of career was in complete conformity with his philosophical position of the period: since both history and philosophy were over, it made sense to abandon them and to serve the French state that he deemed universal.

However Kojève vacillated on the question of when exactly history ends. At a certain moment he had some expectations of the Stalinist state, but later (1948–1958) he related the end of history to the American way of life with its universal consumption. In the note already cited, he writes the following:

I was led to conclude from this that the 'American way of life' was the type of life specific to the post-historical period, the actual presence of the United States in the world prefiguring the 'eternal present' future of all of humanity. Thus, Man's return to animality appeared no longer as a possibility that was yet to come, but as a certainty that was already present. (161)

This idea concerning the beginning of the end of time is perhaps the best known since it was popularized in the work of Francis Fukuyama, who associates the end of history with American liberal democracy, or Western capitalism. Kojève, however, in 1959, after actually visiting Japan, completely changed his mind. On observing certain famous Japanese rituals, such as 'the Noh theatre, the ceremony of tea, and the art of bouquets of flowers', he realized that man can even go so far as to commit 'a perfectly "gratuitous" suicide' beyond the Western logic of the struggle for recognition, political, social and other historical values, 'from pure snobbery', the pure enjoyment of the beauty of the form of this very gesture. *No animal can be a snob*, averred Kojève as he went so far as to reject the very idea of the death of man and related the end of history to this formal, 'snobbish', 'Japanese' perspective:

'Post-historical' Japanese civilization undertook ways diametrically opposed to the 'American way'. No doubt, there were no longer in Japan any Religion, Morals, or Politics in the 'European' or 'historical' sense of these words. But snobbery in its pure form created disciplines negating the 'natural' or 'animal' given which in effectiveness far surpassed those that arose, in Japan or elsewhere, from 'historical' Action – that is, from warlike and revolutionary Fights or from forced Work. … This seems to allow one to believe that the recently begun interaction between Japan and the Western World will finally lead not to a rebarbarization of the Japanese but to a 'Japanization' of the Westerners (including the Russians). Now, since no animal can be a snob, every 'Japanized' post-historical period would be specifically human. (161–162)

Thus, finally, in making his choice between the man and the animal, Kojève decided in favour of the man, the Japanese, the one who instead of returning to the animal condition gives himself up to the free play of forms, which are now liberated from their contents. As Kojève writes in the same footnote,

To remain human, Man must remain a 'Subject opposed to the Object' even if 'Action negating the given and Error' disappears. This means that while henceforth speaking in an *adequate* fashion of everything that is given to him, post-historical Man must continue to detach 'form' from 'content', doing so no longer in order actively to transform the latter, but so that he may oppose himself as a pure 'form' to himself and to others taken as 'content' of any sort. (162)

Thus, what remains after the end of history, the remnant, is not an animal, but, on the contrary, it is precisely what is most human in man; and what is human in man is in fact not history, not politics, nor battle, but his fundamental *formal* opposition, as *subject*, to some *objective content*. After the end of history, this opposition is finally free of the 'noise' of time, since the form is purified of the contingency of content. History brings humanity to the state of pure formalism, to the kingdom of pure art. One might notice that here Kojève directly contradicts his initial hypothesis that at the end of time everything dies together – history, philosophy, man, art. Step by step, this affirmation is dismantled and man redeemed through the partisan insistence of art, although he changes his nature by eradicating the content.

The Man without Content is the title of a book by Agamben devoted to art. Speaking of Hegel, Agamben points out that in fact he never assumed that art was dead or finished with, but that art transcends itself and goes beyond itself by its self-negation, and that the 'self annihilating nothing' is in a way embodied by a certain pure gesture of art, which is rather incapable of dying:

> If we now ask ourselves again, so what about art? What does it mean that art points beyond itself? We can perhaps answer: art does not die but, having become a self-annihilating nothing, eternally survives itself … Its twilight can last more than the totality of its day, because its death is precisely its inability to die, its inability to measure itself to the essential origin of the work. Artistic subjectivity without content is now the pure force of negation that everywhere and at all times affirms only itself as absolute freedom that mirrors itself in pure self-consciousness. (Agamben 1999: 56)

In this book Agamben takes up an essential Hegelian reference to Diderot's *Rameau's Nephew* that introduces the figure of 'the man of taste' as a perversion indicating not so much the end of art as the new capacity, historically acquired by the human, to grasp the proper value or to estimate the quality of the work of art. The man of taste historically replaces the man of art. What disappears is the position of the artist as a creator, or, to put it in Nietzschean terms, as a will to power, an active, desiring, violent producer, that is the man in historical sense. What appears is the position of the spectator, the one who contemplates with disinterest, the Kantian observer. It is not by chance that, according to Hegel, this figure emerges at the time of the French Revolution, which was the first Kojèvian 'endpoint'.

> On the verge of the French Revolution, this particular perversion of the man of taste was taken to an extreme by Diderot in a short satire that, having already been translated into German by Goethe at the manuscript stage, exerted a powerful influence on the young Hegel. In the satire, Rameau's nephew is a man of extraordinary good taste and at the same time, a despicable rascal. In him every difference between good and evil, nobility and commonness, virtue and vice has disappeared: only taste, in the middle of the absolute perversion of everything into its opposite has maintained its dignity and lucidity ... In Rameau's nephew taste has worked like a sort of moral gangrene, devouring every other content and every other spiritual determination, and it exerts itself, in the end, in a total void. (Agamben 1999: 22)

The new capacity of the man of taste is clearly related to the autonomy of aesthetic judgement, introduced by Kant, but also to the idea of knowledge. The man of taste knows what is good and bad when it comes to art; he has achieved a kind of knowledge that now makes him unable to act, to produce art, for 'he does not find any sense of what is essential, because every content and every moral determination has been destroyed' (ibid.) – he can only make his judgements about it.

But, after all, the man of taste is not all what remains after the end of history (which Agamben sees not as post-apocalyptic, but as messianic). Something else emerges there. At the very beginning of *The Open*, Agamben refers to a miniature from a Hebrew Bible from the thirteenth century, found in the Ambrosian Library of Milan, which represents a messianic banquet of the righteous on the last day, who seat with crowned heads 'at a richly laid table'. Agamben pays attention to one detail in particular:

> beneath the crowns, the miniaturist has represented the righteous not with human faces, but with unmistakably animal heads. Here, not only do we recognize the eschatological animals in the three figures on the right, the eagle's fierce beak, the red head of the ox, and the lion's head, but the other two righteous ones in the image also display the grotesque features of an ass and the profile of a leopard. And in turn the two musicians have animal heads as well-in particular the more visible one on the right, who plays a kind of fiddle and shows an inspired monkey's face. (Agamben 2004: 2)

This image is described in the very first chapter of Agamben's book on the animal. The second chapter refers to Georges Bataille, and the third to Kojève and his idea of post-historical snobbery. Agamben pretends to believe in the Kojèvian story about the end of times, but when trying to answer the question of the remnant, he makes a different choice. In a nutshell, what remains after the end of history, according to Agamben, is actually the animal, but this animal is precisely the most intriguing part of the entire drama. It is not so much a consumerist human animal, but rather a kind of sabbatical animal – from the night of his profound boredom a messiah will come. In opposition to Kojève, life rather than death is Agamben's greatest concern. Animal life, bare life and the eternal messianic life are endowed with the same ontological status, which is extremely high. Agambenian animal life is a vitalist response to the Kojevian obsession with death. The characteristics of Agambenian life shift from the bare and the animal to the messianic and the divine –rest, eternity, the sabbath, the end of work.

If we turn to Bataille, we will see that, in his own response to Kojève, which was actually one of the first objections to the idea of the end of history, and which sounded as a lone and desperate voice, seemingly unheard by Kojève, he also talks about life. But this is another life, which does not know rest. Basically, his objection amounts to the following: 'history is over, but *what about me*?' In his *Letter to X, Lecturer on Hegel*, written in 1937, Bataille famously writes as follows:

If action (doing) is – as Hegel says – negativity, the question arises as to whether the negativity of one who has 'nothing more to do' disappears or remains in a state of 'unemployed negativity'. Personally, I can only decide in one way, being myself precisely this 'unemployed negativity' (I would not be able to define myself more precisely). I don't mind Hegel's having foreseen this possibility; at least he didn't situate it at the conclusion of the process he described. I imagine that my life – or, better yet, its aborting, the open wound that is my life – constitutes all by itself the refutation of Hegel's closed system. (Bataille 1997: 296)

What remains, according to Bataille, is thus 'the open wound' of his life as a negativity which still persists (precisely, as he explains, in the work of art) but of which there is supposedly no need. The humanity of the human, which has already been thrown away, is nothing more than the obscene refuse of desire. Bataille suggests that for Kojève this leftover would be merely a 'misfortune', like an 'underdeveloped' country supposedly lagging behind in its historical progress: 'What I am saying about it encourages you to think that all that takes place is just some misfortune, and that's all. Confronted with you, my self-justification is no different from that of a howling animal with its foot in a trap' (297).

However, we should not be trapped and fooled by Bataille's 'me'. In fact, his overly present 'me' is being put into play as a conceptual persona for negativity. There is nothing really personal in this person, nothing individual. He says 'my life', but he explains, 'Really, the question is no longer one of misfortune, or of life, but only of what becomes of "unemployed negativity"' (ibid.).

At first it seems that, in Bataille, negativity cannot be applied to animality, since Bataille is one of those philosophers who draw a line of distinction between humans and animals,[3] and unemployed negativity is precisely what remains of the human being after the end of history and what prevents the end of history from finally being consummated or completed (moreover, it is perhaps thanks to Bataille's intervention that Kojève, who at first pretended to ignore his argument, finally moved away from the idea of an animality which remains after the end, towards art and the properly human, the pure form). Laughter, play, eroticism, the arts, religion and other forms of activity associated with transgression and unproductive expenditure beyond the machinery of labour and production are described by Bataille as intrinsically human moments of sovereignty and autonomy. This approach clearly derives from Kojève, and certainly not from Hegel, for whom, as is made clear in the *Philosophy of Nature*, negativity, even though it is very much employed, is clearly presented not only in the animal kingdom but also in the whole of nature. (It is very important to note that Kojève completely rejected Hegel's *Philosophy of Nature* for its 'absolute idealism' and the spiritualization of matter; Bataille refers only to the *Phenomenology of Spirit* in Kojeve's interpretation.) Yet there is a way to turn Bataille on his head – by addressing his understanding not of the end, but of the *beginning of history*.

First of all, the 'open wound' in the human being is produced by a voluntary negation of its 'animal nature'. Thus, when we speak of a borderline between human and animal in Bataille, we have in mind such phenomena as eroticism, which goes hand in hand with the awareness of death, language and productive labour. Eroticism, according to Bataille, is essentially a sexual activity of humans which stands opposed to animal sexuality, the latter being an ordinary biological phenomenon, a kind of spontaneous, immediate behaviour on the part of an individual in its natural environment. Bataille claims that, while humans surround their lives with restrictions, rules, laws, rituals and prohibitions, animals do not have a law to transgress; they just enjoy, without shame, their unlimited sexual freedom: 'If there is a clear distinction between man and animal, it is perhaps sharpest here: for an animal, nothing is ever forbidden' (Bataille 1955: 31).

This mechanism of the production of human identity through detachment from animality (by way of prohibition) and this explanation of negativity as an exceptionally human phenomenon look very Kojèvian, and the only thing that saves Bataille from this is the fact that he considers this detachment, on the one hand, from a historical perspective, as something which has happened, and, on the other hand, as something impossible, as nothing but a fake or a comedy. Paradoxically, this detachment, in spite of its counterfeit character, is at the same time ontologically meaningful, and of course, very painful, in so far as the boundary between the human and the animal passes through the human body. At the beginning, according to Bataille, there was an event of separation from animality. This is what Bataille calls 'the first step' of the human. This first step is irreversible – we cannot 'return to nature'.

But this idea of 'the first step' comprises one of the biggest paradoxes in Bataillean anthropology, which even Bataille himself did not manage altogether to come to grips with: in fact, it is not a *human*, but an *animal* that negates itself. This is the very first historical, or rather prehistorical, negation. One should here consider how, in *Tears of Eros*, Bataille describes the first man as he begins to practise funeral rites:

> However, these men who were the first to take care of the corpses of their kin were themselves not yet exactly humans. The skulls they left still have apelike characteristics: the jaw is protuberant, and very often the arch of the eyebrows is crowned by a bony ridge. These primitive beings, moreover, did not quite have that upright posture which, morally and physically, defines us – and affirms us in our being. Without doubt, they stood upright: but their legs were not perfectly rigid as are ours. It even seems that they had, like apes, a hairy exterior, which covered them and protected them from the cold. (Bataille 1989: 25)

In order to become the only animal which negates itself as an animal, this creature had first to be an animal, which, suddenly, for some reason, rises, straightens its legs and says, 'I am not an animal any more'. At this point Bataille turns out to be much more Hegelian than Kojève, without being aware of it for the simple fact that Bataille's Hegel is Kojève's. What he considers, following Kojève, as *human* in a human animal might rather be understood as the *animal* in the human animal, that which appears precisely as negativity, in retrospective anticipation. How can we not compare, in this regard, the Bataillean prehistoric man depicted in Lascaux 'beneath an animal mask' with the Agambenian post-historical righteous with animal heads? As Brett Buchanan suggests,

Is it not possible, then, that the passage from animality to humanity is either still underway, never to be completed, or, in what might be the same thing, was always doomed from the start to be a failed passage? Might not the transgression of the boundary separating humanity and animality be not against animality per se, but against the idea that animality had been left behind in the thought of our birth? If this is the case – and admittedly it is only a wild hypothesis – then the paintings in Lascaux depict the acknowledgement of being always already prehuman, or, put otherwise, that humanity is a condition that is never fully formed inasmuch as it is a process continually in the making. (Buchanan 2011: 15)

A certain symmetry between the prehuman and the post-human, Bataillean unemployed negativity and Agambenian sabbatical life, brings us back to another aspect of the Bataillean animal, which was mentioned before with respect to his analysis of the paintings in Lascaux, and which refers us to the animal's sovereignty and actual unemployment. Animals do not work; according to Bataille, they are sovereign. In his short essay 'Friendship of a Man and a Beast' (Bataille 1988: 167–171), he says that while some beasts do, of course, work for men, they are not completely employed, but rather pretend to be so. One should specify here that this even applies to the whole army of domestic, agricultural and other animals, employed by humans: they work, but they remain unpaid. Our very survival is based on animal slavery, the animal body being a perfect subject of exploitation, a labour force in its pure bodily form.

But for Bataille, even when animals labour, they remain strangely detached from it, as if secretly retaining their sovereignty. They have a kind of potentiality to stop working at any moment, like a horse all of a sudden galloping off. If they get carried away, we will never stop them. Bataillean animals enjoy their sovereignty without knowing that they do. But his human animals, too, can experience this kind of sovereignty, for example, proletarians or philosophers, when they stop working and negate their unfreedom through the simple act of drinking wine. Such sovereignty is not that of the monarch but rather that of the beast. In the *Theory of Religion*, he describes a sovereign moment of his own wine-drinking:

> Now I place a large glass of alcohol on my table.
>
> I have been useful. I have bought a table, a glass, etc.
>
> But this table is not a means of labor: it helps me to drink alcohol.
>
> In setting my drinking glass on the table, to that extent *I have destroyed the table*, or at least I have destroyed the labour that was needed to make it …
>
> Had I just once seized the moment by the hair, all the preceding time would already be in the power of that moment seized. And all the supplies, all the jobs that allowed me to do so would suddenly be destroyed; like a river, they would

drain endlessly into the ocean of that brief instant. (Bataille 1992: 102)

In his book *Sovereignty*, Bataille writes about workers, who are, in a way, paradoxically, closer to freedom, then bourgeoisie, possessed by its possessions, precisely because of their alienation of labour together with its means and its products. A useless glass of wine gives to the worker a miraculous, glorious moment.

If I consider the real world, the worker's wage enables him to drink a glass of wine: he may do so, as he says, to give him strength, but he really drinks in the hope of escaping the necessity that is the principle of labour. As I see it, if the worker treats himself to the drink, this is essentially because into the wine he swallows there enters a miraculous element of savour, which is precisely the essence of sovereignty. It's not much, but at least the glass of wine gives him, for a brief moment, the miraculous sensation of having the world at his disposal. The wine is downed mechanically (no sooner swallowed than the worker forgets it), and yet it is the source of intoxication, whose miraculous value no one can dispute. (Bataille 1991: 198)

The excess of sovereignty brings Bataillean animals, philosophers and workers back to Hegelian negativity, which expresses itself particularly in the Eleusinian mysteries 'of the eating of bread and the drinking of wine': it may be experienced by any subjectivity including the animal, which violently negates things by devouring them. It seems that unemployed negativity, which Bataille posits on the side of the human – laughter, eroticism, play – still comes from this abandoned, desperate animal. Those who want to finalize history should first of all send this animal away. Otherwise they will get what Marx calls the subject of History – its highest, culminating point, the point of negation and self-negation of the proletarian, whom, as Marx says, political economy knows only as a working animal, 'the same as any horse' (Marx 2009: 7–8).

However, one should keep in mind that such a figure of unemployed animality results from my own partisan reading of Bataille against Bataille, since for Bataille himself there is still a very important difference between the immediate sovereignty of the animal and the restless negativity of the human, even though sometimes this difference is rendered ambiguous or indistinct. If we want to understand this difference, we need to consider following a digression that will lead us to another aspect of animality in philosophy, namely the permanent association between animality and immanence.

6

Dialectics of the fish

'Animality is immediacy and immanence' (Bataille 1992: 17), Bataille writes in the *Theory of Religion*, commenting on the animal kingdom in general and comparing it with the human world, which is distinguished by a thoroughgoing mediation and negativity. At this point, Bataille is close to Heidegger, according to whom, 'throughout the course of its life the animal also maintains itself in a specific element, whether it is water or air or both, in such a way that the element belonging to it goes unnoticed by the animal' (Heidegger 1995: 292). Bataillean animality does not know negation or rupture, and maintains itself in the continuity of life. As emphasized by Benjamin Noys, in Bataille, 'the world of animals is a world without difference because animals know nothing of negativity, and thereby know nothing of difference' (Noys 2000: 136).

It is all right, for Bataille, if one animal devours the other, since it does not clearly differentiate itself from its prey (there is no other here). Both, eating and being eaten, share some pulsation: the generosity of life is easily transformed into the exuberance of death. 'Every animal is in the world like water in water' (Bataille 1992: 19). Does this metaphor not make us think of fish, almost imperceptibly gliding somewhere between the waves? As Carrie Rohman has pointed out, one may suspect that when he formulated this 'reductionist definition of animal ontology' (Rohman 2009: 95), Bataille could actually have had in his hand a beautiful poem by D.H. Lawrence, *Fish*:

> Fish, oh Fish,
> So little matters!
> Whether the waters rise and cover the earth
> Or whether the waters wilt in the hollow places,
> All one to you.
> Aqueous, subaqueous,
> Submerged
> And wave-thrilled.
> As the waters roll
> Roll you.
> The waters wash,
> You wash in oneness
> And never emerge. (Lawrence 1995: 105)

Rohman explains as follows: 'Fish have a privileged experience of immanence, since their milieu is contiguous, ubiquitous water …. The fish is literally "In the element,/No more"' (Rohman 2009: 96). In order to understand how this can ever be possible, we have to segue into a brief excursus on the political ontology of fish. Surprisingly or not, it is precisely the fish who almost invisibly and silently accompanies a large part of philosophical reflection. The fish is, so to speak, negatively presented in the margins of metaphysics. This creature has often been taken as a peripheral, yet obscenely typical example of a being living in its own element or environment, namely water. The silent fish gliding through water appears as the very image of immanence, of the animal's conformity to its natural essence. Philosophers always speak of fish when they want to talk about the essence of animal being: the picture of water as the element *par excellence* with a fish swimming stupidly in it is entirely convincing.

One of the culminating points of the immanence of fish can be found in Deleuze and Guattari, for whom an unlimited becoming of elements is the very production of the abstract machine of the cosmos. Deleuze and Guattari took the animal as a positive example of the ontology of affirmation,[1] the very model for becoming, raising it from the bottom of the subhuman to the very apex of the philosophical universe. In the chapter of *A Thousand Plateaus* entitled 'Becoming Intense, Becoming Imperceptible', there is the most beautiful and least banal philosophical hymn to the fish that one can found:

Becoming everybody/everything [*tout le monde*] is to world [*faire monde*], to make a world [*faire un monde*]. By process of elimination, one is no longer anything more than an abstract line, or a piece in a puzzle that is itself abstract. It is by conjugating, by continuing with other lines, other pieces, that one makes a world that can overlay the first one, like a transparency. Animal elegance, the camouflage fish, the clandestine: this fish is crisscrossed by abstract lines that resemble nothing, that do not even follow its organic divisions; but thus disorganized, disarticulated, it worlds with the lines of a rock, sand, and plants, becoming imperceptible. The fish is like the Chinese poet: not imitative or structural, but cosmic. (Deleuze and Guattari 2005: 280)

'Making world' or the worlding of the fish seems like a peculiar inversion of the cosmic picture of Leibniz's *Monadology*. What in Deleuze and Guattari becomes 'disorganised, disarticulated', in Leibniz is still 'cultivated', the order of the universe of monads protected against any chaos or confusion.

Each portion of matter may be conceived of as a garden full of plants, and as a pond full of fishes. But each branch of the plant, each member of the animal, each drop of its humors is also such a garden or such a pond. And although the earth or air embraced between the plants of the garden, or the water between the fish of the pond, is neither plant nor fish, they yet contain more of them, but for the most part so tiny as to be to us imperceptible. Therefore there is nothing uncultivated, nothing sterile, nothing dead in the universe, no chaos, no confusion except in appearance. Just as a pond would appear from a distance in which we might see the confused movement and swarming, so to speak, of the fishes in the pond, without perceiving the fish themselves. (Leibniz 1890: 228)

Everything is all right; there is no reason for anxiety: this mantra should be repeated at the high point of thought, because this is removed from an abyss of insanity and ultimate confusion by the merest of steps. Not that Deleuze and Guattari recommend taking this step, but they proclaim that nomads should supersede monads. The elements of the world are no longer closed in on themselves but constantly moving, crossing borderlines, and becoming those very borderlines between themselves and themselves as others.

The image of water becomes rather disturbing when Deleuze and Guattari introduce the figure of a monster – Moby-Dick. The Deleuzian Moby-Dick is 'neither an individual, nor a species … but a phenomenon of bordering' (Deleuze and Guattari 2005: 245). He is 'anomalous' – the one through which passes the borderline between one 'pack' and another, the point of affect where a certain multiplicity changes its nature. Deleuze quotes Melville's Ahab: "'To me, the white whale is that wall, shoved near to me". The white wall. "Sometimes I think there is naught beyond"' (ibid.). Through his becoming-whale, Ahab is trying to pass through this white wall of the animal becoming a colour, 'pure whiteness' (this becoming will bring him to his death).

Deleuzian animals are immanent to such an extent that they know death in a way totally different from humans: 'In contrast to what is said, it is not the human beings, who know how to die, but the animals' (Deleuze 2010).

In Andrei Platonov we find a brilliant illustration of the human jealousy over the animal which is supposed to know how to die, presumably possessing the ultimate wisdom of life and death.

Zakhar Pavlovich knew one man, a fisherman from Lake Mutevo, who had questioned many people about death and who was melancholy from his curiosity; this fisherman loved fish not as food, but as special beings that probably knew the secret of death. He would show the eyes of a dead fish to Zakhar Pavlovich and say, 'Look – true wisdom! A fish stands between life and death, and that's why he's mute and stares without expression. I mean even a calf thinks, but not a fish – it knows everything already'. (Platonov 1978: 26–27)

Platonov's character, in following the fish, is trying to penetrate its secret, the secret of death:

Zakhar Pavlovich tried to talk him out of it: 'There's nothing special there, just something cramped'. A year after that, the fisherman couldn't bear it anymore and threw himself into the lake from his boat, having tied his feet with a rope so that he wouldn't start to swim accidentally. In secret he didn't believe in death at all, the important thing was that he wanted to look at what was there – perhaps it was much more interesting than living in a village or on the shores of a lake; he saw death as another province, located under the sky, as if at the bottom of cool water, and it attracted him. Some of the muzhiks the fisherman talked with about his intention to live with death for a while and return tried to talk him out of it, but others agreed with him: 'True enough, Mitry Ivanich, nothing ventured, nothing gained. Try it, then you'll tell us'. Dmitry Ivanich tried: they dragged him from the lake after three days and buried him by the fence in the village graveyard. (ibid.)

The becoming-fish of the fisherman aims to place him astride the threshold of death (almost like the white whale for Captain Ahab). But the fisherman cannot divide himself in two parts – death and survival – in such a way that somebody, like an inner 'human being', would still exist in order to observe his animal body dying.

It makes no difference whether the fish does or does not know the difference between life and death: such is its way of existence, which philosophers usually call 'immanence'. Imagine a fish suddenly becoming jealous of some human beings sitting on the beach and talking about the politics of animal emancipation and tries to come ashore from the water and join in the conversation. One might object that the process of evolution cannot run so fast, even though such things do indeed happen in the history of nature and some fish really do leave the water, creeping out and starting to get a feel for the earth (the case of Darwin). Others argue that evolution simply cannot take place at all (the case of Hegel).

For a Hegelian fish it is better to just stay in the water, if they want to correspond to their notion and not present 'a sorry picture' like those whales, reptiles, amphibians and aquatic birds, suspended in between water, air and earth. However, Hegelian immanence is ambiguous and even self-contradictory. The Hegelian animal, as a form of subjectivity, manifests its freedom in its own way, in its anxiety, unhappiness and unrest. Yes, whales and other monsters are all sorry pictures and shameful mistakes of nature, but one can also discern the great demonic figure of Moby-Dick, the anomalous, rising behind Hegel's back.

According to Catherine Malabou, who in the wonderful article 'Who's Afraid of Hegelian Wolves?' criticizes the Deleuzian reading of Hegel; the latter is himself the anomalous of *Deleuze*'s philosophy:

> My question is as follows: does not Hegel, inasmuch as he incarnates in the extreme a 'normal' unity, become Deleuze's 'anomalous', the unavoidable and indispensable 'phenomenon of bordering' the packs that run in all directions through his text? ... Deleuze and Guattari write: 'wherever there is multiplicity, you will also find an exceptional individual ... There may be no such thing as a lone wolf, but there is a leader of the pack, a master of the pack, or else the old deposed head of the pack now living alone, there is the Loner, and there is the Demon' (Deleuze and Guattari 2005: 243). By dint of being designated in such a haunting, insistent, obsessive way, as adequate to itself, rule, or law (*nomos*), does not Hegel's name end up by setting itself apart from those of all other philosophers, by exceeding them as leader of the pack or their 'anomalous'? (Malabou 1996: 120)

I would like, however, to take one more step here and argue that this subjective perspective is not enough to describe what I call the 'negative animal'. An unrest emanating from within the living being is still not enough to really push the animal beyond itself. A fish can become anxious yet still stay in the water: water remains water, and fish remains fish. Even a fundamental anxiety cannot prevent the animal's reconciliation with reality. A fish will hardly leave the water just because it wants to express itself in a way other than swimming, such as joining a human conversation. But there are certain conditions – let us call them 'external', or 'objective' – in which immanence becomes impossible. Let us address to *The German Ideology*, where Marx and Engels' criticize Feuerbach for his 'misunderstanding of existing reality', which comes from the view that the existence of something is its essence and that 'the conditions of existence, the mode of life and activity of an animal or human individual are those in which its "essence" feels itself satisfied'. If someone or something is not satisfied by their conditions of existence, this is, according to this view, an exception and an 'unhappy chance'. On this, Marx and Engels reply:

> Thus if millions of proletarians feel by no means contented with their living conditions, if their 'existence' does not in the least correspond to their 'essence', then, according to the passage quoted, this is an unavoidable misfortune, which must be borne quietly. The millions of proletarians and communists, however, think differently and will prove this in time, when they bring their 'existence' into harmony with their 'essence' in a practical way, by means of a revolution. (Marx and Engels 1976: 58)

And here comes the fish:

> The 'essence' of the fish is its 'being', water .... The 'essence' of the freshwater fish is the water of a river. But the latter ceases to be the 'essence' of the fish and is no longer a suitable medium of existence as soon as the river is made to serve industry, as soon as it is polluted by dyes and other waste products and

navigated by steamboats, or as soon as its water is diverted into canals where simple drainage can deprive the fish of its medium of existence. (59)

As we can see, Marx and Engels' fish brings something completely new, something that draws a connection between animals, proletarians and communists. The essence does not coincide with the existence; nothing coincides with itself (this is already a Hegelian lesson). History creates itself from this non-coincidence, and this shift can be read not as an 'unhappy chance' but as a necessity. If there is something wrong with Hegel's *Philosophy of Nature*, then it may be his prescription for all natural forms to stick to their respective notions, a prescription which, in fact, keeps nature from entering the realm of history such that the contradiction between the two tends towards the 'bad infinity' of mutual distortion. A silent riot of Marxian fish denotes the necessity and urgency of revolution as a universal change. The uneasiness of a single creature in the world is not a problem only for this particular creature but for the world itself, in so far as it is becoming unbearable. One might object that 'fish cannot make a revolution', but do we really know whether proletarians can? The very topic of revolution is all about impossibility, which itself is never absolute, but which recognizes itself as a possibility only retrospectively, by bestowing a meaning and a necessity upon what was previously a mere contingency.

Overcoming impossibility as a historical necessity – that is what is already inscribed in the logic of Hegelian becoming. If we look back we can see that the menagerie of spirit is ready to explode at any moment, since it is inhabited by a multiplicity of all those unhappy, anxious and negative creatures. However, until this many-voiced crowd of Hegelian amphibians, birds, slaves and southern people use this opportunity for subjectivity and therefore rush to this cleft opened by the despair, anxiety and unrest of every something, every anything, this metaphysical unit named 'man' will make – particularly with Heidegger – another attempt to draw again a definite demarcation line between itself and the animal other.

7

The shepherd of being

The Heideggerian animal is, indeed, an immense topic, which has been thoroughly explored by contemporary thought.[1] As is well known, Heidegger's intention was, among others, to do away with all previous humanist anthropology. However, his opposition to anthropologism, according to his own definition,

> does not mean that such thinking aligns itself against the humane and advocates the inhuman, that it promotes the inhumane and deprecates the dignity of the human being. Humanism is opposed because it does not set the *humanitas* of the human being high enough. (Heidegger 1998: 251)

Leaving behind a broad metaphysical tradition of thinking the human as an animal *plus something else*, for instance, as an animal with reason or a rational animal, which means to think the human in relation to its animal nature, Heidegger claims that the human being is not an animal at all, that the human and the animal are actually two different forms of being, that their distinction is nothing less than ontological. As he writes in his

Letter on Humanism, 'The human body is something essentially other than an animal organism' (ibid.). It is closer to the gods, 'standing in the clearing of being', and, Heidegger goes on: 'Such standing in the clearing of being I call the *ek-sistence* of human beings. This way of being is proper only to the human Being' (ibid.).

Moreover man himself 'is the "there" [*Da*], that is, the clearing of being' (248), and is exposed to truth in its openness, whereas animals simply live with no relation to truth. Between man and animal, there is an abyss:

> In any case living creatures are as they are without standing outside their being as such and within the truth of being, preserving in such standing the essential nature of their being. Of all the beings that are, presumably the most difficult to think about are living creatures, because on the one hand they are in a certain way most closely akin to us, and on the other they are at the same time separated from our *ek-sistent* essence by an abyss. However, it might also seem as though the essence of divinity is closer to us than what is so alien in other living creatures, closer, namely, in an essential distance that, however distant, is nonetheless more familiar to our *ek-sistent* essence than is our scarcely conceivable, abysmal bodily kinship with the beast. (ibid.)

Heideggerian animals live their life, but they do not *ek-sist*. Plunged into their natural environment, they remain captive to this environment: 'Throughout the course of its life the animal is confined to its environmental world, immured as it were within a fixed sphere that is incapable of further expansion or contraction' (Heidegger 1995: 198).

Any of a given animal's movements, being motivated by a certain lack, like hunger, always brings the animal back to itself. This closed circular movement does not presuppose a way out, but presents a kind of missed encounter with the external world, which cannot be possessed by the animal as man possesses it. 'The animal is poor in world' (186).

A decisive part of Heidegger's *Fundamental Concepts of Metaphysics* is dedicated to the animal's poverty, exploring the question of what it means to be poor in world, passing through an analysis of the animal organism, behaviour, capacities, drives, through a reading of historical and contemporary biologists (Hans Dreisch, Jakob von Uexküll and others), by means of a comparison between the animal (world-poor), the non-organic, the stone (worldless), and the human (world-forming). Poverty determines the animal's mode of being. The animal is poor as it is deprived, whereas we are rich; we have the entire world: 'If poverty implies deprivation then the thesis that "the animal is poor in world" means something like "the animal is deprived of world", "the animal has no world" .... For man does have a world' (196).

Having the world is essential to a human being. We *have* and we *are*, for, in Heidegger, as Derrida emphasizes, '*the property of man*, or the idea of that which is man proper – is inseparable from the question or from the truth of Being' (Derrida 1969: 45). The 'magnetic attraction' of this property, Derrida interprets, following Heidegger, as the idea of man's particular proximity to being. The relations of property, in the Heideggerian world, appear in the clearing of truth; and the clearing of truth, which is, apparently, quite narrow, is already occupied by humans.

However, Heidegger emphasizes, deprivation is a *not-having* that is at the same time a kind of *having*. But this potential of having in the living organism always remains an actual not-having, and this is a true poverty – animals have a limited access to things they need, being unable to experience those things *as* what they are in themselves: they have 'no relation to the "as such" that constitutes truth' (Lindberg 2004: 76), since the manifestation of beings as such, of beings in their being, is given in language and is opened up by language. And what is being after all if not this *is*, which operates in language and which gives being to the entirety of beings expressed by language? As Derrida puts it, '"Being" and language – or the group of languages – which it governs or which it opens, such is the name of that which assures this passage by the *we* between metaphysics and humanism' (Derrida 1969: 42).

So, if we are to understand what it means to be poor in world, we should first understand what the word 'world' means, and, as Heidegger explains in the *Letter on Humanism*, the world is precisely this 'clearing of being':

Because plants and animals are lodged in their respective environments but are never placed freely into the clearing of being which alone is 'world', they lack language … In its essence, language is not the utterance of an organism: nor is it the expression of a living thing. Nor can it ever be thought in an essentially correct way in terms of its symbolic character, perhaps not even in terms of the character of signification. Language is the clearing-concealing advent of being itself. (Heidegger 1998: 248–249)

The abyss between man and his poor relative is thus the abyss of an ontological inequality. This specification clarifies a principle: it is not that animals lack the world because they lack language, but they lack language because they lack the world. It is not only that they do not have language, but they cannot have it; language is not among the animal's capacities – it is among the human's abilities. In contrast to the Franciscan or Hegelian bird which either brings a message from god or manifests its own being, a Heideggerian bird can produce only a meaningless noise:

Given that the 'hearing' is according to Heidegger the very condition of possibility of speech, can the animal's 'noise', its squeal, 'speak' to us: call us, touch us, be addressed to us? … From Heidegger's point of view, the animal might well *express* itself and its sentiments in its voice, yet it could not be *heard* by man – because the essence of speech is not auto-*expression* but a possibility to share a sense. Man doesn't hear what the animal says to him … the gods give sense whereas the animals only make noise. (Lindberg 2004: 76–77)

A fundamental incapacity, which defines the animal's relation to the external world – dumb poverty – was already there before this very relation could appear. The world they have is not a common world, not a common space, but their restricted environment, to which their body naturally conforms. They can never leave their living circle (the 'disinhibiting ring' (*enthemmungsring*) of stimuli to which they have a finite number of innate responses); they always bring it along with them. Heidegger says, '*Language* is the house of *Being*. In its *home* human beings dwell' (Heidegger 1998: 239). By contrast, animals are poor and homeless, silent prisoners. They cannot share the sense of the world in which they live in poverty and solitude (which, in turn, cannot be experienced by them *as* poverty and solitude). Sharing sense, and sharing in general, is attributed by Heidegger to human richness and generosity. The ability to share is inscribed in the very structure of the human body; along with Hegel, Heidegger says that only human beings have hands: 'The hand, along with the word, is the essential mark of the human … no animal has a hand, and a hand never originates from a paw or a claw or a talon' (Heidegger 1992: 118).

Human hands not only use tools, write and produce – they also give and share. Hands are used for gifts. And only humans have a gift – the gift of being, of language, of thought. In Heidegger, as emphasized by Derrida,

> man's hand *gives and gives itself, gives* and *is given* […] like thought or what gives itself to be thought […] whereas the organ of the ape or of a man as a simple animal, indeed as *animal rationale*, can only *take hold of, grasp, lay hands on the thing.* The organ can *only* take hold of and manipulate the thing insofar as, in any case, it does not have to deal with the

thing *as such*, does not let the thing be what it is in its essence. (Derrida 1990: 175)

But maybe we can give them something, offer something with our own hands? In his essay, 'Sloughing the Human', Steve Baker interestingly discusses the problem of Heidegger's hands in the context of art and draws a striking parallel with Beuys' famous performance from 1974, *Coyote: I Like America and America Likes Me*, which was staged in the René Block Gallery in New York. The artist was staying at the gallery space together with the live coyote Little John for one week. Baker pays special attention to one detail: 'In a space strewn with straw, lengths of felt, ripped copies of the *Wall Street Journal*, and a variety of other materials the artist had brought alone, a pair of gloves (which he had painted brown and which he repeatedly threw down to the coyote)' (Wolf 2003: 151).

As explained by Beuys himself, in this performance 'the roles were exchanged immediately' and the coyote appeared as 'an important co-operator in the production of freedom', bringing the artist closer to that which 'the human being cannot understand'.

The brown gloves represent my hands. They have the freedom to do a wide range of things, to utilise any number of tools and instruments. They can wield a hammer or cut with a knife. They can write or mould forms. Hands are universal, and this is the significance of the human hand … They are not restricted to one specific use like the talons of an eagle or the mole's diggers. So the throwing of the gloves to Little John meant giving him my hands to play with. (ibid.)

This example hints not so much at the alterity of the animal for man as at 'the other-than-animal: the human' (ibid.). It interpellates the animal; it calls upon the animal to become human. The artist gives to the animal that which is itself capable of giving – hands. But can the animal respond with a gift in return? In Heidegger – definitely not. It always remains suspended in its living world, and it has no way out. As Susanna Lindberg perfectly explains,

> In *The Fundamental Concepts of Metaphysics*, Heidegger names the kind of a being that can touch the animal its 'disinhibitor' (*Enthemmung*). Less then a sign, the disinhibitor is nevertheless what makes sense to the animal. The disinhibitor breaks the animal's originarily closed and 'inhibited' way of being by opening its environment, even if the animal's comportment towards this openness rests a simple stupefied 'captivation'. [...] Following Jakob von Uexküll, Heidegger considers that an animal's disinhibitors constitute its environment. The environment is not a space *in* which the animal might meet various disinhibitors, but the whole of its disinhibitors *are* its environment and, as such, the points that form its 'outline' or the 'circle' in which the animal moves. An animal's life is its incessant relation with an environment unfolded by its disinhibitors. (Lindberg 2004: 67)

However, there is another possibility in Heidegger; there is another 'unconscious philosopher' lurking there behind the discourse of the openness of *Dasein*. It is in its very 'captivation' that the animal in Heidegger, half closed in its openness, half open in its closedness, becomes a very ambiguous figure. This ambiguity will be radicalized by Agamben, who, in *The Open*, deduces the very essence of *Dasein* from the secretness of unconscious animal life. According to Agamben, the crossing point where animality meets humanity is *profound boredom* as one of the fundamental attunements of *Dasein*, the one that is opposed by Heidegger to 'the essence of animality' (captivation). As Agamben puts it,

> In captivation the animal was in an immediate relation with its disinhibitor, exposed to and stunned by it, yet in such a way that the disinhibitor could never be revealed as such. What the animal is precisely unable to do is suspend and deactivate its relationship with the ring of its specific disinhibitors. The animal environment is constituted in such a way that something like a pure possibility can never become manifest within it. (Agamben 2004: 67–68)

However, there is not only great distance but at the same time also proximity between animal captivation and profound boredom, and this zone of proximity is where a passage from one to another occurs:

> Profound boredom then appears as the metaphysical operator in which the passage from poverty in world to world, from

animal environment to human world, is realized; at issue here is nothing less than anthropogenesis, the becoming Dasein of living man. (ibid.)

Living man takes on a burden of *Dasein* and thus becoming-human. However, this passage does not 'open onto a further, wider, and brighter space, achieved beyond the limits of the animal environment, and unrelated to it' (ibid.). Instead, it suspends the animal relation with its environment and deactivates its disinhibitor. Only due to this deactivation and suspension, animal's captivation can be 'grasped as such'. Agamben links this point to Heidegger's motif of the openness of *Dasein* and 'the neither-open-nor-closed of the animal environment', and claims that thus appears 'an undisconcealed as such, the suspension and capture of the lark-not-seeing-the-open': 'The jewel set at the center of the human world and its *Lichtung* (clearing) is nothing but animal captivation; the wonder "that beings are" is nothing but the grasping of the "essential disruption" that occurs in the living being from its being exposed in a nonrevelation' (ibid.).

Agamben continues this analysis with a reference to Heidegger's course on Parmenides:

Heidegger insists several times on the primacy of *lethe* with respect to unconcealedness. The origin of concealedness (*Verborgenheit*) with respect to unconcealedness (*Unverborgenheit*) remains so much in the shadows that it could in some ways be defined as the originary secret of unconcealedness [...] This secret of unconcealedness must be unraveled in this sense: the *lethe* that holds sway at the center of *aletheia* – the nontruth that also belongs originarily to the truth – is undisconcealedness, the not-open of the animal. (Agamben 2004: 68–69)

Thus, Agamben associates animality with the *lethe* of *aletheia*. Truth, *Aletheia*, bears in itself this *lethe* – oblivion, forgetfulness, which in Heidegger turns into the oblivion of being. The animal, therefore, suddenly appears at the very heart of the oblivion of being – not in the sense that the animal is the one who has 'forgotten' it, but rather in the sense that the animal is precisely what was forgotten. It seems that Agamben creates a new monster out of Heideggerian *Dasein* – an ontological animal. And indeed, to continue in this vein, which may seem absurd only at first sight, let me take a famous Heideggerian metaphor literally and read it as a direct statement: if 'the human being is the shepherd of being' (Heidegger 1998: 252), then *being is a herd*.

Is it not that the very *call of being*, which Heidegger is trying to discern in its oblivion, echoes the non-articulated animal voice, in which the philosopher hears only a meaningless sound? Is it not that the call comes from the animal-being, lost and forgotten by its shepherd? And is this not the same as the non-articulated voice of the animal that confronts its own violent death, which, in Agamben (in his reading of Hegel), anticipates the appearance of the human?

This move cannot but evoke once again the demon of retrospection, which has already appeared – in different guises –

in Kafka, in Hegel, in Freud, but also elsewhere. Thus, Lacan, in his interpretation of Freud's Wolf Man case, in *Seminar I*, comes to the 'amazing' conclusion that the repressed and repression are the same thing:

> The trauma, in so far as it has a repressing action, intervenes *after the fact [après coup], nachträglich*. At this specific moment, something of the subject's becomes detached in the very symbolic world that he is engaged in integrating. From then on, it will no longer be something belonging to the subject. The subject will no longer speak it, will no longer integrate it. Nevertheless, it will remain there, somewhere, spoken, if one can put it this way, by something the subject does not control [...]. Repression begins, having constituted its original nucleus. (Lacan 1991a: 191)

This statement provokes an intriguing discussion between Hyppolite and Lacan about the Heideggerian play of *lethe* and *aletheia*, of oblivion and truth, in its relation to the practice of psychoanalysis. This discussion takes its departure from Octave Mannoni's question about 'successful repression', or 'successful symbolic integration', which, according to Lacan, 'always involves a sort of normal forgetting' (192).

> LACAN: Integration into history evidently brings with it the forgetting of an entire world of shadows which are not transposed into symbolic existence. And if this symbolic existence is successful and is fully taken on by the subject, it leaves no weight behind it. One would then have to bring in

Heideggerian notions. In every entry of being into its habitation in words, there's a margin of forgetting, a *lethe* complementary to every *aletheia*.

HYPPOLITE: It is the word *successful* in Mannoni's formula that I don't understand.

LACAN: It is a therapist's expression. Successful repression is essential.

HYPPOLITE: *Successful* could mean the most profound forgetting.

LACAN: That is what I am talking about.

HYPPOLITE: So this *successful* means, in certain respects, total failure. To arrive at the integration of being, man must forget the essential. This *successful* is a *failure*. Heidegger would not accept the word *successful*. You can only say *successful* from the therapist's point of view.

LACAN: It is a therapist's point of view. Nonetheless, the margin of error there is to be found in every realisation of being is always, it seems, reserved by Heidegger for a sort of fundamental *lethe,* or shadow of the truth.

HYPPOLITE: The therapist's success – nothing could be worse for Heidegger. It is the forgetting of the forgetting. Heideggerian authenticity consists in not being engulfed by the forgetting of the forgetting.

LACAN: Yes, because Heidegger made a sort of philosophical law out of this return to the sources of being. (ibid.)

For the retrospective animal, there is nowhere to return, since the 'source', the truth and the sense of its animal being – as anticipation of freedom – but at the same time the 'trauma' which opened up the gap between the present and the past – intervenes after the fact. From this gap, a profound boredom emerges and eventually constitutes what we are.

And, again, Kafka states,

> He no longer has even his old vocation, indeed He has forgotten what he once represented. Probably it is this very forgetting that gives rise to a certain melancholy, unrest, a certain longing for vanished ages, darkening the present. And yet this longing is an essential element in human effort, perhaps indeed human effort itself. ('He', *Notes from the Year 1920*, Bloom 2003: 64)

Vladislav Sofronov, in his book on love, quotes the last phrase of this note as one example among others of what he calls the *animal of thought* (Sofronov 2009: 38). The animal of thought is the figure which Sofronov introduces in order to designate an affective dimension of thought, the 'it thinks' of a bodily subject. The animal here, however, is not 'a beastie', or 'a little beast', but rather an 'aggregate state' of thought (akin to solid, liquid and gas) (48). The animal is an aggregate state of a desperate subject in love, a thinker *and* an animal, which, instead of sublimation, jumps into a kind of phenomenological reduction. The animal of thought is the most refined – not among animals, but among thoughts.[2]

8

Poor life

The Russian word for 'boredom' is *toska*. In his book *Affective Mapping: Melancholia and the Politics of Modernism*, in the chapter dedicated to Andrei Platonov, who uses this word very frequently, Jonathan Flatley attempts a definition of this 'paradigmatic' Russian 'untranslatable':

> The Oxford Russian-English Dictionary translates *toska* as 'melancholy, torment, longing, depression', but as Vladimir Nabokov has noted, 'no single word in English renders all the shades of *toska*'. Like 'melancholy', *toska* has a rich connotative field. Nabokov gives a sense of its range: 'at its deepest and most painful, it is a sensation of great spiritual anguish, often without any specific cause. At less morbid levels it is a dull ache of the soul, a longing with nothing to long for, a sick pining, a vague restlessness, mental throes, yearning. In particular cases it may be the desire for somebody or something specific, nostalgia, lovesickness. At the lowest level, it grades into ennui, boredom'[1] …

While its range and usage are in some way similar to the English 'melancholy', *toska* can take an object in a way that neither depression nor melancholia (at least in current usage) can. While one can be depressed or melancholic *about* something, this does not suggest the same active feeling in relation to an object as is indicated by having *toska for* something (home, a friend, socialism). ... Relatedly, *toska* has a verb form. As a verb, the word underscores the potentially and paradoxically active nature of lacking something. (Flatley 2008: 160)

To this very exhaustive explanation, I would just add that *toska* can express an active feeling not only *for* something but *against* something, or, to be precise, against a certain given situation, against everything in general: quite often *toska* indicates the situation which a subject finds absolutely unbearable. In this case, *toska* sounds as a call for action; it refers to the urgency, to the immediate necessity for a total change (otherwise the situation will remain unbearable). It can designate the anticipation of a sudden negative interruption.

In this last sense, the Russian word *toska* has nothing to do with Heideggerian nostalgia. This particular kind of profound boredom does not care about the source of being. It is the suffering which cannot let things be. In this chapter I will address Andrei Platonov's writings in order to show that this boredom can underlie nature's very desire for change, which is inscribed in the poverty of animal life and which, in a way, affects a revolutionary utopia. In a word, I will put the Russian Revolutionary writer, who shares with Heidegger some basic concepts, like profound boredom and the poverty of the animal, in a kind of virtual dialogue or polemic with the German counter-revolutionary philosopher.[2]

Among the many intellectuals, artists, poets and writers who were inspired by the Russian Revolution and invested a great deal of creative energy and work in it, Andrei Platonov is a unique figure. Being of industrial proletarian descent, he became a major Russian writer for whom the revolution was to consist in crafting a truly Marxist literary practice, firmly focused on the topics of community, sexuality, gender, labour, production, death, nature, utopianism and the paradoxes of creating a new (and better) future.

However, his extraordinary writing was 'forgotten' twice. First, as a result of Stalinist censorship, which rejected Platonov because of his deviation from the general line of 'social realism'. (His best works were composed 'for the drawer' and published only years after his death.) Second, by later liberal and religious interpretations of his complicated prose as yet another ironic allegory of 'real socialism'. Nevertheless, Platonov's works have been a point of reference for such thinkers as Georg Lukács, Fredric Jameson and Slavoj Žižek. In Russia, too, a new wave of authors is trying to rethink Platonov's writings, applying to them new theoretical instruments and hoping to liberate their initial political challenge from the rough ideological shell in which it is enclosed.

In this chapter, I aim to reveal Platonov's animality[3] as part of his tragic dialectic of nature and as an expression of his messianic expectations for the epoch of the Russian Revolution.[4] For this, I intend to develop an interpretation of Platonov's idea of a *poor life* in a concrete politico-ontological perspective. Platonov wrote a great deal on life and its poverty. *Poor life* is the life of animals and plants, but also of people who build happiness and communism precisely out of this life. Poverty is a condition in which life is supposed to be the main or even the only possible material resource, a universal substance of existence, which is used in the production of everything. Everything that is great, revolution included, is also to be produced from out of this poor, weak substance: 'a human being comes out of a worm' (Platonov 1989: 378).

In contrast to Heidegger, for whom the animal is an embodiment of poor life, as opposed to the human being, *Dasein*, whose essence is finitude and death and who possesses all the wealth of the world and therefore has an ontological predominance over animals, Platonov is clearly on the side of those small, poor and weak living beings, and he attributes to them a certain inner virtue of existence:

> Surely not every animal and plant could be sad and wretched; this was a dream or pretense of theirs, or some temporary disfigurement they were suffering from. Otherwise one would have to assume that true enthusiasm lies only in the human heart – and such an assumption is worthless and empty, since the blackthorn is imbued with a scent, and the eyes of a tortoise with a thoughtfulness, that signify the great inner worth of their existence, a dignity complete in itself and needing no supplement from the soul of a human being. (Platonov 2008: 120)

The idea that living beings have inner worth makes Platonov look closely at the most trifling creatures and find in them a kind of spirituality on the part of matter itself. Yes, animal life is poor in world, but the world itself is even poorer and is unquestionably in need of the energy of this life in order to resist the forces of entropy and death. Such a resistance takes place through labour: animals, plants and impoverished human beings are always working hard to live and enjoy life. In the story 'Among Animals And Plants' (1936), he thus describes a baby hare:

> The same chubby little baby hare was burrowing in the earth with his paws, trying to dig out some rootlets or a cabbage leaf that had been dropped on the ground last year. The hare's concern for his own life was inexhaustible, since he needed to grow and his desire for food was continuous. After eating whatever was there in the ground, the hare defecated a little and played with his tail. He then began to bat one of his paws with the other three; after that he played with the remains of some dead bark, with bits of his own droppings and even with empty air, trying to catch it between his front paws. Finding a puddle, the hare had a good drink, looked all around with moist, conscious eyes, lay down in a little pit to one side, curled up into the warmth of his own body and dozed off. He had already tasted all the delights of life; he had eaten, drunk, breathed, inspected the locality, felt pleasure, played about a bit and fallen asleep. (Platonov 2008: 159)

In his novel, *Soul*, which I will analyse more in detail later, someone enters the grass, and the reader discovers a secret exuberance of life there.

The plants round about trembled, shaken from below as all kinds of unseen creatures tried to escape from him – some on stomachs, some with tiny legs, some through low-level flight, each doing what it could. Until then they had probably been sitting there silently, but only a few had been sleeping – certainly not all of them. Each was so burdened with tasks that there was evidently not enough day for them – or else they felt it was a pity to expend their brief lives in sleep and so were just barely dozing, lowering a membrane halfway over each eye so they could see at least half of life, hear the darkness and forget the needs of daytime. (Platonov 2008: 22)

The first characteristic of poor life is *diligence*. Platonov's animals, plants and impoverished human beings are *working* to maintain their lives. The second characteristic – and this is already intrinsically animal – is *generosity* and its ability to *give*, to make a gift. If Heideggerian animals cannot give, but only take or grab, not only because they are poor and therefore have nothing to give but also because they do not have hands, then in Platonov only poor life has the ability to give, whereas richness amounts to greediness – the rich only take and appropriate more and more.

Poor life has neither possessions nor hands to give, but it generously shares itself, and animals give to humans their life substance, their 'soul', together with their flesh. In this respect, they are close to the sacrificial animals of Georges Bataille, although the Bataillean animal is described in terms of the expenditure of the excess of nature, whereas Platonov's animal is described in terms of misery and lack. Numerous scenes of eating meat in Platonov recall strange sacrificial rituals, operating in a regime of extreme economy:

> When his father brought birds and animals back with him, he had eaten them thriftily and sensibly, teaching his children to do the same, so that an extinguished gift of nature would be transformed to man's benefit and not to go waste down the latrine. He used to say that the meat and bones of dead creatures should do more than just fill you up; they should also provide you with a good soul, and strength of heart and reason. If you can't take from a bird or an animal its most valuable good, if all you want is a full stomach – then eat vegetables, eat cabbage soup, or bread crumbled in water. His father held that the world's animals and birds were precious souls, and that love for them was sound husbandry. (Platonov 2008: 157–158)

> We had a cow. While she lived, my mother, my father and I all ate milk from her. Then she had a son – a calf – and he drank milk from her too, there were three of us and he made four, and there was enough milk for us all. The cow also ploughed and carried loads. Then her son was sold for meat, he was killed and eaten. The cow was very unhappy, but she soon died from a train. And she was eaten too, because she was beef. Now there is nothing. The cow gave us everything, that is her milk, her son, her meat, her skin, her innards and her bones, she was kind. (Platonov 1999: 148)

Would one or two birds be enough for them to eat their fill? No. But their sad longing might turn into joy if each of them was given a tiny pinch of flesh from a bird. This trifling morsel of flesh would serve not so much to fill them up as to reunite them with life in general and with one another; its grease would oil the creaking, withering bones of their skeletons; it would give them a feeling of reality, and they would remember that they existed. Food at this moment would serve both to nourish the soul, and to make empty, submissive eyes begin to shine again and take in the sunlight scattered over the earth. (Platonov 2008: 92)

Animal flesh in Platonov serves for 'feeding the soul' and at the same time gives to the body its own 'good soul'. The human soul is thus eating the animal body, while the human body is eating the animal soul. Platonov's soul, which eats flesh and which feeds the body, is material; it has nothing to do with the incorporeal Christian soul, ascending to heaven after death. It is an *anima*, the matter of life, which is one of the names for the substance circulating among bodies, from animal to human and between humans themselves. A life substance goes from one body to another through eating or, for example, in moments of intimacy, of sexual excitation between lovers or emotional proximity between friends. Such moments can have a deep existential meaning, which finds witty expression in Platonov's essay 'Anti-Sexus' (1926), where Charlie Chaplin, in his reply to an advertisement for a new masturbatory device, comments as follows:

I'm against the Anti-Sexus. It doesn't allow for intimacy, for the living interaction of people's souls, but it's this interaction that's always foremost whenever the sexes unite, even in those cases when the woman is a commodity. This interaction has its own value, independent from sexual intercourse: it's that fleeting feeling of friendship and sweet affinity, that feeling of your loneliness melting away, that no antisexual mechanism can give. I'm for the actual closeness of people, for them breathing into each other's mouths, for one pair of eyes gazing straight into another, for how you truly feel your own soul during the crude act of intercourse, and for enriching it at the expense of some other soul that just happened along. This is why I'm against the Anti-Sexus. I'm for the living, suffering, laughable, stuck-in-a-rut human being who blows his stock of meager life-juice just to feel a moment of fraternity with another derivative being. (Platonov 2013: 51–52)

Platonov's animals, even though they are poor and tired due to the hard work of maintaining their life, are nevertheless very open to sexual enjoyment. It is in no way random that Henry Ford, Chaplin's opponent on the 'Anti-Sexus', proposes to the producers of the device of auto-satisfaction that they should distribute their commodity among the 'planet's entire animal population' (51). The smaller the animal, the shorter its life span, but the greater its voluptuousness and excitement: facing imminent death,[5] even the most insignificant, 'derivative being' hurries to love the other one and thus participate, with all of its poor, weak forces, in a kind of universal movement of life.

Further on were reeds, and when Chagataev entered them, all their inhabitants began to call out, fly up or fidget about where they were. It was warm in the reeds. Not all the birds and animals had been scared away by this man; judging by the sounds and voices, some had remained where they were – so frightened that, thinking their end was near, they were now hurrying to reproduce and find pleasure. Chagataev knew these sounds from long ago; and now, listening to the weak, agonizing voices from the warm grass, he felt sympathy for all poor life that refuses to give up its last joy. (Platonov 2008: 22)

However, there is a difference between the passions of Platonov's animals and the passions of man. Humans suppress their immediate sexual desire and sometimes their abstention approaches an extreme condition, whereas animals are rather unlimited. Animal passion and desire consist in following their nature as a destiny, which does not know any alternative; this is why their suffering, love, anxiety, hunger and anger cannot find respite unless it is in immediate satisfaction or death.

Chagataev was certain of this; he knew the direct, unbearable feelings of wild animals and birds. They cannot weep and so find comfort for themselves, and forgiveness for their enemy, in tears and in exhaustion of heart. They can only act, wanting to wear out their suffering in combat, inside the dead body of their enemy or in their own destruction. (Platonov 2008: 89)

The cow was not eating anything now; she was breathing slowly and silently, and a heavy, difficult grief languished inside her, one that could have no end and could only grow because, unlike a human being, she was unable to allay this grief inside her with words, consciousness, a friend or any other distraction. ... The cow did not understand that it is possible to forget one happiness, to find another and then live again, not suffering any longer. Her dim mind did not have the strength to help her deceive herself; if something had once entered her heart or her feelings, then it could not be suppressed there or forgotten. (Platonov 1999: 144)

Adorno and Horkheimer, who in their *Dialectic of Enlightenment* write about the absence of conceptual thinking in animals, point out that precisely because of this absence, animals experience the strongest possible *suffering*. (The authors posit this in opposition to Descartes' famous assertion that animals *do not suffer*.) In a way, this corresponds to Platonov's sensibility towards animality. In Adorno and Horkheimer, too, animals cannot resist their destiny, which is natural need (and therefore they actually resemble the unhappy Hegelian beasts).

Deprivation of comfort does not secure an animal alleviation of fear; or unconsciousness of happiness any respite from pain and sorrow. If happiness is to materialize, bestowing death on existence, there must be an identifying memory, a mitigating cognition, the religious or philosophical idea – in short, a concept. Happy animals there are, but then how short-lived is their happiness! The life of an animal, unrelieved by the liberating influence of thought, is dreary and harsh. Escape from the dismal emptiness of existence calls for resistance,

and for this speech is essential. Even the strongest of animals
is infinitely weak. (Adorno and Horkheimer 1989: 246–247)

The infinite weakness of animals that 'cannot apply the brake of
cognition to their destiny' (247). Their unhappiness and suffering
does not know pause, and continues because it does not know the
dialectics of reason with its moments of discursive interruption. In
Platonov, the law of animal life is inscribed in another dialectics –
the *dialectics of nature*. The tragedy of this dialectic consists in the
cruelty of life, adhered to in death, when some have to be eaten
by others. Thus, in *Soul*, Platonov describes the so-called 'sheep
circle': sheep are wandering across the desert in search of some
grass, people are pursuing the sheep and predators and dogs are
going after the people, eating those who die.

At noon old Sufyan took Chagataev aside, away from the dry
path, and told him that, around the channels of Amu-Darya,
one could still happen upon two or three old sheep that lived
on their own and had quite forgotten human beings except
that, if they saw a man, they would remember their shepherds
from long ago and come running up to him. These feral sheep
had survived by chance; they were all that remained of the
enormous flocks that the beys had tried unsuccessfully to take
with them into Afghanistan. And for several years the sheep
had lived in the desert with their sheep dogs; the dogs had
taken to eating the sheep, but then the dogs had all died or run
away in melancholy yearning, and the sheep had been left on
their own, gradually dying of old age, or being killed by wild
beasts, or straying into waterless sands. A few, however, had

survived and were still wandering about, trembling beside one another, afraid of being left on their own. They wandered in huge circles over the impoverished steppe and never left their circular path, thereby giving evidence of a vital good sense – blades of grass that the sheep had eaten, or trampled down, were able to grow again before the sheep had gone all the way around and come back to where they had been before. Sufyan knew of four such grassy circles that these remnants of feral flocks continued to wander around till their death. One of these circuits lay not far away, almost intersecting the track which the Dzhan nation was now following towards Sary-Kamysh. (Platonov 2008: 63)

He knew many wild beasts and birds that ate dead people in the desert. Probably wild animals were silently following the nation all the time keeping at an invisible distance and eating those who fell. Sheep, the Dzhan nation, and wild animals – this triple procession was moving in orderly fashion through the desert. But the sheep sometimes strayed from their grassy path and followed a wandering tumbleweed as it was driven about by the wind – and so the universal guiding force, of everything from plants to humans, was really the wind. (76)

There is, however, not only tragedy in nature but also hope. And this hope is kept alive thanks to the very same poor life that feeds a thirsty animal and looks out from within its body with intelligent human eyes. There is a hidden human being imprisoned inside every one of Platonov's animals. Thus, a character in his novel *Rubbish Wind* suddenly recognizes a dog as a former human.

In the morning a dog came fearfully to the rubbish pit, like a beggar woman. On seeing the dog, Lichtenberg immediately understood that it was a former man who had been reduced by grief and need to the senselessness of an animal, and he did not frightened it any more. But the dog began to tremble with horror as soon as it noticed the man; its eyes moistened over with deathly sorrow; terror sapped its strength and it was only with difficulty that it vanished. (Platonov 1999: 79)

Platonov is able to read from animal faces and their gaze the suffering and hopes of a sad and unknown human being who cannot even cry or express its sadness in any other way. The description of the mute suffering of the camel in *Soul* is one of the most insistent:

As he came to the dried-up bed of the Kunya-Darya, Nazar Chagataev saw a camel sitting like a human being, propped up on his front legs in a drift of sand. He was thin, his humps had sagged, and he was looking shyly out of black eyes, like a sad and intelligent human being. … The camel then closed his eyes, because he did not know how he was meant to cry. (Platonov 2008: 26)

Platonov's animal is a man in disguise, tortured by his unrecognized intellect, imprisoned in his natural body. While, in his *Letter on Humanism*, Heidegger writes of an insuperable abyss separating animals from humans, the protagonist of Platonov's *The Sea of Youth* (a novel written in 1934 but forbidden by Soviet censorship and published only in 1986) thinks that the gap between humans and other beings has to be overcome by means of a communist revolution, which must prolong, if not accelerate, Darwinian evolution and, thus, ultimately liberate animals from their very animality as a form of insanity. 'We should change the world as soon as possible', proclaims one of its characters, 'because even animals are already becoming insane' (Platonov 1990a: 294).

Here, from a historical perspective, I should clarify that, after the October Revolution of 1917, the standards of a 'revolution in nature' and even of a 'struggle against nature' were continually raised in all spheres of the nascent Soviet society. Nature was supposed to have changed, being both liberated from its reliance on necessity and preserved from the precariousness of its contingency. A diffuse avant-garde attitude unconditionally sustained the idea of a point of no return, an 'abandon ship!', a total transformation of the social and natural order towards emancipation and equality. Nature was also considered a battlefield for class struggle. A potential or an actual transformation of one species into another – for instance, animals into humans – accompanied by the acquisition of higher levels of consciousness and freedom, is the theme that runs throughout the Soviet literature and poetry of the period and can be characterized as revolutionary humanism.

This immediately seems to be to adopt a clearly anthropocentric perspective, perhaps inherent to emancipatory voluntarist politics, which shows its tendency to end up reproducing the very structures of inequality, state and power that it was designed to replace. But this is not to privilege the opposite utopia of deep ecology based on the idea of going back to wonderful nature, which is supposedly authentic and free. Neither does it privilege contemporary vitalist projections, which endow forms of life themselves with enough force to resist any institutional repressive apparatuses. Nature is not 'nice': the Russian revolution sees it, in a Hegelian-Marxist spirit, in terms of unfreedom, suffering and exploitation, and the animal kingdom serves as a kind of model of a society that should be transformed. It is not a matter of the predominance and superiority of one species over another, but a matter of taking everything into account. In so far as inequality between species remains untouched, the equality of people, too, can never be achieved. Or, to put it otherwise, if, according to Adorno, there can be animals without dialectics, there is no dialectics without animals. As emphasized by Marco Maurizi, who investigates the topic of animals and dialectics, especially in Adorno, history is the history of oppression, and a violent domination of humans by humans begins with the human domination of nature (Maurizi 2012: 67–103).

'I see the liberties of horses/and equal rights for cows', writes the futurist poet Velimir Khlebnikov (Khlebnikov 2008: 181). Nikolay Zabolotsky, one of the founders of the Russian avant-garde absurdist group OBERIU, in his poem *The Triumph of Agriculture*, describes nature as suffering under the old bourgeois regime, compares animals with proletarians and creates a utopia involving their progressive liberation facilitated by technology.

I saw a red glow in the window
Belonging to a rational ox.
The parliament of ponderous cows
Sat there engaged in problem-solving.
...
Down below the temple of machinery
Manufactured oxygen pancakes.
There horses, friends of chemistry,
Had polymeric soup,
Some others sailed midair
Expecting visitors from the sky.
A cow in formulas and ribbons
Baked pie out of elements
And large chemical oats
Grew in protective coats. (Zabolotsky 2005)

Platonov deserves a special attention in this respect. In his writings, it is not only human beings but all living creatures, including plants, that are overwhelmed by the *desire for communism*, a desire which, as Fredric Jameson has pointed out, has still not found its Freud or Lacan (Jameson 1994: 97).[6] A passage from *Chevengur* (1928–1929) is emblematic in this regard: 'Chepurny touched a burdock – it too wanted communism: the entire weed patch was a friendship of living plants [...]. Just like the proletariat, this grass endures the life of heat and the death of deep snow' (Platonov 1978: 198).

The desire for communism arises from profound boredom (*toska*) and the unbearableness of the existing order of things. In his own way, Platonov, too, is trying to think through the ways of change, the 'struggle against nature' by means of technology, in all its ambiguity. He writes in his small essay titled, 'On Socialist Tragedy':

Nature is not great, it is not abundant. Or it is so harshly arranged that it has never bestowed its abundance and greatness on anyone. This is a good thing, otherwise – in historical time – all of nature would have been plundered, wasted, eaten up, people would have revelled in it down to its very bones; there would always have been enough appetite. If the physical world had not had its one law – in fact, the basic law: that of the dialectic – this would have sufficed for people to have destroyed the world completely in a few short centuries. More: even without people, nature would have destroyed itself into pieces of its own accord. The dialectic is probably an expression of miserliness, of the daunting harshness of nature's construction, and it is only thanks to this that the historical formation of humankind became possible … The situation between technology and nature is tragic. The aim of technology: 'give me a place to stand and I will move the world'. But the construction of nature is such that it does not like to be beaten. … Nature keeps itself to itself, it can only function by exchanging like for like, or even with something added in its favour, but technology strains to have it the other way around. The external world is protected from us by the dialectic. Therefore, though it seems like a paradox: the dialectic of nature is the greatest resistance to technology and the enemy of humankind. Technology is intended for and works towards the overturning or softening of the dialectic. So far it has only modestly succeeded, and so the world still cannot be kind to us. At the same time, the dialectic alone is our sole instructor and resource against an early, senseless demise in childish enjoyment. Just as it was the force that created all technology. (Platonov 2011: 31–32)

Platonov's expectations towards communism thus go far beyond ideology and politics. The more depressive and tragic nature is, the stronger the hope for happiness and freedom. This hope is essential, and it possesses all the force of natural life with its passion, which in animals consists in following their destiny without knowing any alternative besides death.

Platonov's communists and Bolsheviks are revolutionary animals. They literally recognize themselves in animals' faces and project onto animals their own revolutionary passion. And if, like human beings, they are ascetic and refuse an immediate gratification of bodily desires, they do it because their greater desire or their really unbearable desire is the desire – and *toska* – for communism. They are moved by their passion for the realization of happiness for everyone, including the smallest animals.

The desire for communism or socialism is neither a sublimation nor a sublation nor a discursive interruption of sexual desire or whatever natural need. Quite the opposite – it is a kind of debauchery. The necessity and urgency of revolution as a planetary change is already inscribed in the unconscious animal nature, which seems to expect from humans, from communists, from *us*, a kind of salvation. Platonov's historical materialism is moved by the force of an anxious animal's intolerance of all that is and by the happy anticipation of all that should be.

> The desert's deserted emptiness, the camel, even the pitiful wandering grass – all this ought to be serious, grand and triumphant. Inside every poor creature was a sense of some other happy destiny, a destiny that was necessary and inevitable – why, then, did they find their lives such a burden and why were they always waiting for something? (Platonov 2008: 28)

In this perspective, revolution is not so much a move forward as an absurd gesture of turning 'back' – towards these weak, forgotten creatures who are awaiting help. As Mayakovsky writes in his *Ode to Revolution*, 'You send sailors/To the sinking cruiser/ There where forgotten/Kitten was crying.' The only problem is that it is always already *too late*. It seems as if poor life lacks the very life that it needs in order to actualize itself, to realize itself as a destiny and to seize upon its small, unique chance. This chance is more often recognized only when it is already lost, as in the moments when animals are dying. Life, for Platonov, is a losing and lost possibility. Each time the death of the animal witnesses this chance as lost testifies to the fact that we were too late. The tragedy of his animality consists in the fact that an impossible catastrophe happens at every moment. The animal dies of sorrow and misery without achieving its long-awaited happiness, and man is left alone with his mourning.

Lastly he saw a small tortoise. No longer preserving herself beneath her armor, she lay with her little feet sticking out helplessly and with a swollen, protruding neck; she had died here by the side of the road. Chagataev picked her up and examined her. He carried her away to one side and buried her in the sand. (Platonov 2008: 57)

Mourning functions as an internalizing or keeping of what is lost. Memory is a faithful thought: by keeping the lost, the one who remembers saves it from the emptiness of oblivion. Memory is a fidelity to what is not there any more, but what nevertheless endows us, as Walter Benjamin famously says in his Thesis II on the Philosophy of History, with 'weak Messianic power'.

The past carries with it a temporal index by which it is referred to redemption. There is a secret agreement between past generations and the present one. Our coming was expected on earth. Like every generation that preceded us, we have been endowed with a weak Messianic power, a power to which the past has a claim. That claim cannot be settled cheaply. Historical materialists are aware of that. (Benjamin 2007b: 254)

The claim of the Benjaminian past is that it affects the present and relates it to the urgency of a revolutionary action, which can answer to the hope that was interrupted by death. If the chance of life was lost, if the creature, in whose heart unknown happiness was beating, still died in poverty, sadness and slavery, then only those who are alive are able to live up to his expectations. Platonov shares with Benjamin this paradoxical view of the materialist dialectics of history, when, for example, he writes about the responsibility of the living before those who died during the war: 'The dead have no one to trust except the living, – and we should live now in such a way, that the death of our people was justified and redeemed through the happy and free destiny of our nation' (Platonov 1984: 109).

In these notes, Platonov identifies himself with a certain nation, and the dead, too, are part of this nation. However, mostly in his prose, he does not describe some actual, existing nation, but rather, to put it in Deleuzian terms, he 'invents a people' (Deleuze 1997: 4), similarly to Kafka, who invents a Mouse Folk. It is no coincidence that Žižek, in his reflection on communist utopia, compares, with reference to Jameson, Platonov and Kafka.

> Fredric Jameson was right to read *Josephine* as Kafka's socio-political utopia, his vision of a radically egalitarian communist society – with the singular exception that Kafka, for whom humans are forever marked by superego guilt, was able to imagine a utopian society only among animals. (Žižek 2010: 370)

It is very important to distinguish such utopian community from the image of some really existing unites of people endowed with all symbolic attributes of a nation. As Deleuze claims,

> This is not exactly a people called upon to dominate the world. It is a minor people, eternally minor, taken up in a

becoming-revolutionary. Perhaps it exists only in the atoms of the writer, a bastard people, inferior, dominated, always in becoming, always incomplete. Bastard no longer designates a familial state, but the process or drift of the races. I am a beast, a Negro of an inferior race for all eternity. (Deleuze 1997: 4)

It is precisely to this kind of bastard people that Platonov dedicates his novel *Soul*, which I have already discussed. Its protagonist, Nazar Chagataev, who trained as an economist in Moscow, is instructed by the party to go to the desert and find there 'a small nomadic nation, drawn from different peoples and wandering about in poverty' (106) in order 'to teach it socialism'. Soul (*Dzhan*) is a generalized personification of the Soviet people, as well as an unexpected metaphor for the Jews (wandering in the desert in search of freedom) and, after all, a literary figure, which gathers under the name of a 'nation' all the unhappy and lost humans and animals.

The nation included Turkmen, Karakalpaks, a few Uzbeks, Kazakhs, Persians, Kurds, Baluchis, and people who had forgotten who they were. ... *The poverty and despair of the nation was so great* that it looked on this work, which lasted for only a few weeks of the year, as a blessing, since during these weeks it was given naan bread and even rice. At the pumps the people did the work of donkeys, using their bodies to turn the wooden wheel that brings water to the irrigation channels. A donkey has to be fed all through the year, whereas the workforce from Sary-Kamysh ate only for a brief period and would then up and leave. And it did not die off entirely;

and the following year it would come back again, after languishing somewhere in the lower depth of the desert.

'I know this nation', said Chagataev. 'I was born in Sary-Kamysh'.

'That's why you're being sent there', the secretary explained. 'What was the name of the nation – do you remember?'

'It wasn't called anything', said Chagataev, 'though it did give itself a little name'.

'What was this name?'

'Dzhan. It means *soul*, or *dear life*. The nation possessed nothing except the soul and dear life given to it by mothers, because it's mothers who give birth to the nation'.

The secretary frowned, and looked sad. 'So there's nothing they can call their own except the hearts in their chests – and even that's only for as long as the hearts keep on beating'.

'Only their hearts', Chagataev agreed. 'Only life itself. Nothing belonged to them beyond the confines of their bodies. But even life wasn't really their own – it was just something they dreamed'.

'Did your mother ever tell you, who the Dzhan are?'

'She did. She said they were runaways and orphans from everywhere, and old, exhausted slaves who had been cast out. There were women who had betrayed their husbands and then vanished, fleeing to Sary-Kamysh in fear. There were young girls who came and never left because they loved men who had suddenly died and they didn't want to marry anyone else. And people who didn't know God, people who mocked

the world. There were criminals. But I was only a little boy –
I can't remember them all'. (Platonov 2008: 25, emphasis
added)

Nation here is a kind of 'substance', matter, which can build
communism out of itself, but which can also exhaust itself as a
natural resource: the poorer the life of the people is, the more
greed it provokes, since nothing prevents its reduction to a pure
labour force. The poor can always be forced to work. That is why
in this nation one is 'afraid of life'.

It has lost the habit of life and it doesn't believe in life. It
pretends to be dead – otherwise those who are happy and
strong will come to torment it again. The Dzhan have kept
almost nothing for themselves, only what nobody else needs,
so that nobody becomes greedy when they see them. (106)

Poor life imitates death. The life of this small population is
disappearing; it literally disappears in the sands of the desert
together with the naked or almost naked people (dressed only in
rags). Platonov narrates the history of this people beginning from
this zero level of life, or, as Agamben would put it, from the grey
zone between life and death. This life is not properly human; it is
deprived of symbolic, real and cultural wealth. It has nothing to
identify with and cannot defend itself from exploitation, which,
according to Platonov, exhausts the living soul.

Chagataev knew from childhood memory, and from his
education in Moscow, that any exploitation of a human
being begins with the distortion of that person's soul, with

getting their soul so used to death that it can be subjugated; without this subjugation, a slave is not a slave. And this forced mutilation of the soul continues, growing more and more violent, until reason in the slave turns to mad and empty mindlessness. (2008: 103)

This is how Platonov inverts the dialectics that from Hegel to Marx claimed that labour transforms an animal into a man and a slave into a master. The Hegelian slave changes the world with his labour and acquires self-consciousness, whereas Platonov's human-animal works to maintain its life and hopes for a better world, but finally exhausts itself and falls into despair, paradoxically finding its last refuge in the dumb body of an animal.

Platonov's escape route from the human is described in his novel *Rubbish Wind*, written in 1934. Its main character, Albert Lichtenberg, a physician of cosmic space, is little by little being transformed into an indefinite animal, being unable to remain human in fascist Germany. He finds his last refuge in this animal body, which no one can recognize any more. And while in *The Sea of Youth*, zoo technician Visokovsky dreams that 'the evolution of the animal kingdom, stopped in former times, will recommence, and all poor creatures, being covered with hair, who are now living in distemper, will finally achieve the fate of a conscious life' (Platonov 1990a), in *Rubbish Wind* we see the inverse process[7]: a man becoming covered in hair and losing his sanity, and then being put into a concentration camp as he is no longer human enough.

Lichtenberg was not asked any questions in the camp office, but only examined – on the assumption that he could hardly be a human being. To cover all eventualities, however, they sentenced him to life imprisonment, writing on his papers: 'A possible new species of social animal, developing a layer of hair, extremities debilitated, sexual attributes poorly defined; this subject, now removed from social circulation, cannot be ascribed to a definite gender; judging by superficial characteristics of the head – a cretin; speaks a few words, pronounced with no apparent animation the phrase, "Supreme half-body Hitler", then stopped. Confined for life'. (Platonov 1999: 79–80)

The judge announced to Lichtenberg that he was sentenced to be shot – on account of the failure of his body and mind to develop in accordance with the theories of German racism and the level of State philosophy, and with the aim of rigorously cleansing the organism of the people of individuals who had fallen into the condition of an animal, so protecting the race from infection by mongrels. (80)

Paradoxically, this unrecognized animal, or animalized man, or, to put it in Agambenian terms, this *muselmann* (Agamben 2002), performs a feat at the end of the story – he saves a Jewish communist woman and helps her escape from the camp, and then finally sacrifices himself in vain, trying to feed with his own meat an insane woman who has lost her child. He exhausts himself to the extent that when his wife, who is looking for him with a police officer, in the end finds his dead body, she cannot recognize it as human.

Out there Zelda saw an unknown animal that had been killed and left, eyes down. She prodded it with her shoe and thought it might even have been a primitive man who had grown a coat of hair, but that most likely it was a large monkey someone had mutilated and then, as a joke, dressed up in scraps of human clothing.

The policemen followed Zelda out and confirmed her guess that it was a monkey or else some other unscientific animal for which Germany had no use; it had probably been dressed up by some young Nazis or Stahlhelms, as a political gesture.

Zelda and the policemen left the empty settlement, where the life of a human being had been lived to the end, with nothing left over. (Platonov 1999: 89)

***

Rubbish Wind is one of the most hopeless of Platonov's writings, where he inverts the entire picture and opens up – for a moment – the secret world of the human being with distemper, which is hidden inside an animal body. He is writing for this dying creature – as, in Deleuze's terms, 'one writes for dying calves' – in order to fix the possibility that was not recognized and is already lost. The human is becoming animal and then finally becoming waste, in a manner similar to Kafka's Gregor Samsa in *Metamorphosis*.[8] What is recognized is the animal. 'Like a dog' – these are the last words of K. in *The Trial*. When someone drives a knife into his heart, he says, 'Like a dog'. To these words Kafka adds, 'It was as if the shame of it was to outlive him.'

Commenting on this passage, Walter Benjamin relates this shame to Kafka's 'unknown family, which is composed of human beings and animals', and under the constraints of which Kafka 'moves cosmic ages in his writings'. Let me follow the path on which Kafka engages Benjamin, preoccupied with the striking irreducibility of the past, of the forgotten, the path that leads towards the world of animality:

Shame is not only shame in the presence of others, but can also be shame one feels for them. ... Kafka did not consider the age in which he lived as an advance over the beginnings of time. His novels are set in a swamp world. ... The fact that it is now forgotten does not mean that it does not extend into the present. On the contrary: it is actual by virtue of this very oblivion. (Benjamin 2007b: 129–130)

What has been forgotten – and this insight affords us yet another avenue of access to Kafka's work – is never something purely individual. Everything forgotten mingles with what has been forgotten of the prehistoric world, forms countless, uncertain, changing compounds, yielding a constant flow of new, strange products. Oblivion is the container from which the inexhaustible intermediate world in Kafka's stories presses toward the light. (131)

The world of ancestors takes Kafka 'down to the animals', which are 'receptacle of the forgotten' (132). Not of *being* as the forgotten, as in Heidegger by way of Agamben (in this case, since being is the linguistic function, a copula, the animal will just positively supplement language with life, and life, as Badiou would put it in his criticism of Deleuze, will be just another name for being (Badiou 2000)), but rather of the forgotten as such, as a meaningful nothingness, around which our being constitutes itself as negativity and memory.

Does that oblivion not derive from the fact that 'I is an other'? If so, this fact, because it cannot but be recognized too late – if at all – endows us with the dramatic and at the same time quite useless knowledge that we are what we have lost. This is an oblivion which is nevertheless constantly pursued by memory. Memory is lurking about the forgotten, restlessly. It is faithful to what is not. The self-relation of the human cannot but confront this paradox – the unhappy animal, which we retrospectively produce out of our own despair, dies ingloriously before we manage to fulfil its anticipation of freedom. Freedom does not coincide with knowledge; neither does it coincide with the humanization of the animal. If 'freedom' – and not an 'escape route' – is Kafka's secret word, if it is everywhere in Kafka's secret world, does this then imply that it is only there and nowhere else?

The drama of the Owl of Minerva is that it always comes too late. As Malabou puts it, 'In its twilight discourse, at the beginning of its night, philosophy may be nothing but the announcement of this truth: it is too late for the future' (Malabou 2005: 4). The Owl of Minerva comes to discover that the gates of the *terra utopia*, where we could realize the last hope of our desperate animality, are already closed. And above these gates it is written:

Truth. Animals are not allowed.

But animals do not know that they are not allowed to enter the gates of truth. They do not care about the gates. Wherever we install a fence to mark a border, the animal will cross it – as the 'only real outlaw'– illegally. After all, to tell the truth, a gate only makes sense for the one who is not allowed to pass through it. The animal will find its escape route precisely where there seems to be no escape. And, potentially, on this route, it will find something else. So, nevertheless, freedom?

Notes

Preface

1 'Benjamin in Palestine: On the Place and Non-Place of Radical Though', Ramallah, 6–11 December 2015.

Introduction

1 The text was written towards the end of 1925, but it was first published decades later. Let me add as a curiosum that, in August 2012, deputy of the Moscow Duma (city parliament) Vladimir Platonov became a kind of 'Anti-Sexus' for his advocacy of the prohibition of all sexual education and propaganda (as detrimental to public health and morality) in Russian public media and schools – from Andrei to Vladimir, this is arguably the most succinct formula of the decay of public life in Russia in the last 100 years.

Chapter 1

1 Thus, Pythagoras' conception is based on the principle of metempsychosis: the element of life – *anima*, immortal soul – passes from one body to another, be it human, animal or plant; Plato in his

Timaeus expounds his mythological conception of a back-to-front evolution, where animals appear as a result of the degradation of the human (Simondon 2011: 32–42).

2 According to Alberto Toscano, Simondon's system of individuation creates a relational ontology, where 'real relations are those relations that co-emerge with their terms' (Toscano 2006: 139).

3 Incidentally, in Deleuze, a good reader of Simondon, the inverse movement in Kafka – human becoming animal, metamorphosis – is interpreted as the same 'living escape route'.

Chapter 2

1 I use the word 'primitive' with some reservation, for what is really primitive is not prehistoric man, but our vocabulary that cannot designate him other than by means of this pejorative term that over the centuries has marked the superiority of 'civilized' man, based on the greater distance the latter is supposed to maintain towards animality.

Chapter 3

1 These two things can be radically different, although they are not necessarily so. Let us respect ambiguity, the mother of paradox: paradise copied nature and was at the same time opposed to it.

2 For the Franciscan roots of Agamben, see Chiesa (2011: 149–163).

3 The fact which, for Bataille, provoked such a delight in prehistoric man.

4 The linkage, which was later rendered unproblematic, transformed into a pure positive statement and was praised by Deleuze and Guattari, especially in their interpretation of the Wolf Man case, as the becoming-animal, multiplicity and animality of the unconscious (see Deleuze and Guattari 2005).

Chapter 4

1 One might compare this with Adorno's famous statement: 'Animals play for the idealistic system virtually the same role as the Jews for fascism' (Adorno 1998: 80).

2 The motif of the human face as the principle of the relation to the other will be later extensively developed by Emmanuel Levinas (Levinas 1979: 187–253).

3 One might note, however, that in contemporary mass culture the most popular image of a human being is the one with an open mouth: thus, most often advertisement shows people with wide smiles, showing their teeth, as if addressing directly to the animal unconscious of consumers.

4 On animality in Hegel, Kojeve and Bataille, see also Timofeeva (2013).

5 'In nature's malleable mirror / The stars – a net, The Gods / – Haunting the dark, fish – are we', writes Velimir Khlebnikov (2008).

6 Agamben cites from Hegel (1932: 212).

7 This will be the eternal messianic life – the life of language, which for Agamben transcends bare life, neither human nor animal. See Chiesa and Ruda (2011: 163–180) for a criticism of Agamben's notion of messianic life.

8 See Buck-Morss (2009) for the interesting analysis of Hegel and real slavery in Western colonies.

Chapter 5

1 On that point, I would rather agree with Fredric Jameson, who claims as follows: 'But I believe that Hegel is here more advanced than Kojève and has more productive clues to offer as to the continuing significance of that "recognition" which Kojève restricted to the interpersonal struggle between Master and Slave' (Jameson 2010: 162).

2 For more on religious and political post-apocalyptic context of Kojeve's ideas, see my article Timofeeva (2014).

3 See Timofeeva (2009). This book, published in Russian, is dedicated to eroticism in Bataille and focuses on animality as a marginal but constitutive figure of Bataillean thought.

Chapter 6

1 See Benjamin Noys' critique of Deleuze's affirmationism: Noys (2010: 51–79).

Chapter 7

1 See, for example, Derrida (2006), Agamben (2004), Lindberg (2004), Atterton and Calarco (2004).

2 'The phrase "the animal of thought" simply means to de-idealize an excess of abstraction in the name of a "thinker". For example, you are taking your belongings from one apartment, where you lived in a building next door to that woman, to the other, rented in another part of the city. And, going down the escalator in the metro, all of a sudden you see that other man – he is going up, towards her, towards the light, on the adjacent escalator. You are coming to your new apartment, thinking, what are they doing there, at her place now, and you are staring at the hook for the chandelier in your ceiling. But at the same time something in you sees this encounter on the escalator as a cinematographic mise-en-scène of the two opposite movements in their pure aesthetics, cinematics, the geometry of the two vectors located around the point-woman. Precisely that which stares at the hook in the ceiling and sees geometry (without leaving the domain of psychology) is the animal of thought' (Sofronov 2009: 33).

Chapter 8

1 Nabokov cited in Pushkin (1991: 141). On the use of *toska,* Flatley also refers Fitzpatrick (2004: 357–371).

2 Here, I would agree with Tora Lane: 'Despite the apparent contrast in thought between the German philosopher, who was profoundly opposed to Bolshevism and the Russian Revolution, and the Soviet writer, whose entire *oeuvre* can be seen as a means of translating the Russian Revolution into literature and keeping its force alive, their thoughts deserve to be brought into dialogue' (Lane 2012: 63). In her article, Lane compares the use of the terms 'ground' and 'groundlessness' in Platonov and Heidegger.

3 See also Günther (2012: 251–272) on Platonov's animals.

4 See also my article on Platonov: Timofeeva (2011).

5 According to the Russian philosopher Valery Podoroga, in Platonov, 'the orgasm represents an instantaneous mode of exchange of energy between intimate bodies under the sign of a growing feeling of death: it is precisely this energy that stimulates desire, whose fulfillment is death' (Podoroga 1991: 355–356). See also his significant and more extended work on Platonov (Podoroga 2011: 239–384).

6 See also Flatley (2008: 180), and my article 'Unconscious Desire for Communism' (Timofeeva 2015a).

7 'The regressive metamorphoses of *Rubbish Wind* suggest that in the fascist "kingdom of appearances" all is not as it seems. In this kingdom of beasts, evolution moves in the opposite direction, i.e. toward a human degradation, and this results in the animalization of man and a racist society that expels defective "subhumans" as extraneous zoomorphic beings' (Günther 2012: 271).

8 See Timofeeva (2015b) for my analysis of Kafka's *Metamorphosis*.

Bibliography

Ades, Dawn and Simon Baker (eds.) 2006, *Undercover Surrealism: Georges Bataille and DOCUMENTS*, Cambridge: MIT Press.

Adorno, Theodor and Max Horkheimer 1989, *Dialectic of Enlightenment*, trans. John Cumming, New York: Continuum.

Adorno, Theodor W. 1998, *Beethoven: The Philosophy of Music: Fragments and Texts*, trans. Edmund Jephcott, Stanford: Stanford University Press.

Agamben, Giorgio 1991, *Language and Death: The Place of Negativity*, trans. P.E. Pinkus and M. Hardt, Minneapolis: University of Minnesota Press.

Agamben, Giorgio 1998, *Homo Sacer: Sovereign Power and Bare Life*, trans. Daniel Heller-Roazen, Stanford: Stanford University Press.

Agamben, Giorgio 1999, *The Man without Content*, trans. Georgia Albert, Stanford: Stanford University Press.

Agamben, Giorgio 2002, *Remnants of Auschwitz: The Witness and the Archive*, trans. Daniel Heller-Roazen, New York: Zone Books.

Agamben, Giorgio 2004, *The Open: Man and Animal*, trans. Kevin Attell, California: Stanford University Press.

Agamben, Giorgio 2013, *The Highest Poverty: Monastic Rules and Form-of-Life*, trans. Adam Kotsko, California: Stanford University Press.

Aristotle 1926, *Nicomachean Ethics*, trans. Harris Rackham, In Aristotle in 23 Volumes, Vol. XIX, Cambridge, MA: Harvard University Press.

Aristotle, 1932, *Politics*, trans. Harris Rackham, In Aristotle in 23 Volumes, Vol. XXI, Cambridge, MA: Harvard University Press.

Aristotle 1974, *Constitution of Athens & Related Texts*, trans. Kurt von Fritz and Ernst Kapp, New York: Hafner Press.

Aristotle, 1991, *History of Animals*, Vol. III, trans. D.M. Balme, In Aristotle in 23 Volumes, Vol. XI, Cambridge, MA: Harvard University Press.

Atterton, Peter and Matthew Calarco (eds.) 2004, *Animal Philosophy: Ethics and Identity*, London: Continuum.

Badiou, Alain 2000, 'Of Life as a Name of Being, or, Deleuze's Vitalist Ontology', trans. Alberto Toscano, *Pli*. 10: 191–199.

Balmès, Francois 2011, *Structure, Logique, Alienation: Recherches En Psychanalyse*, Toulouse: Érès.

Bataille, Georges 1955, *Lascaux, or the Birth of Art*, trans. Austryn Wainhouse, New York: Skira.

Bataille, Georges 1970–88, *Œuvres Completes*: Volume 1–12, Paris: Gallimard.

Bataille, Georges 1985, *Visions of Excess*, trans. Alan Stoekl, Minneapolis: University of Minnesota Press.

Bataille, Georges 1986, 'Metamorphoses', 'Georges Bataille: Writings on Laughter, Sacrifice, Nietzsche, Un-knowing', *October*, 36: 22–23.

Bataille, Georges 1989, *The Tears of Eros*, trans. Peter Connor, San Francisco: City Light Books.

Bataille, Georges 1991, *The Accursed Share: An Essay on General Economy*, in 3 Volumes, trans. Robert Hurley, New York: Zone Books.

Bataille, Georges 1992, *Theory of Religion*, trans. Robert Hurley, New York: Zone Books.

Bataille, Georges 1997, *The Bataille Reader*, Botting, Fred and Scott Wilson (eds.), Oxford: Blackwell Publishing.

Bataille, Georges 2009, *The Cradle of Humanity. Prehistoric Art and Culture*, trans. Michelle Kendall and Stuart Kendall, New York: Zone Books.

Benjamin, Walter 2004, 'Capitalism as Religion', *The Frankfurt School on Religion: Key Writings by the Major Thinkers*, ed. Eduardo Mendieta, London: Routledge.

Benjamin, Andrew 2007a, 'What If the Other Were an Animal? Hegel on Jews, Animals and Disease', *Critical Horizons*, 8: 1, 61–77.

Benjamin, Walter 2007b, *Illuminations*, trans. Harry Zohn, New York: Schocken Books.

Berger, John 2009, *Why Look at Animals?* London: Penguin Books.

Buchanan, Brett 2011, 'Painting the Prehuman: Bataille, Merleau-Ponty, and the Aesthetic Origins of Humanity', *Journal for Critical Animal Studies*, 11: 1–2.

Buck-Morss, Susan 2009, *Hegel, Haiti and Universal History*, Pittsburgh: University of Pittsburgh Press.

Chernoba, Roksolana 2012, *Hermann Nitsch: The Bloody Priest of Vienna*, http://www.desillusionist.com/data/08/04.html. Accessed: 17 October 2017.

Chesterton, Gilbert Keith 2011, *Saint Francis of Assisi*, Nashville: Sam Torode Book Arts.

Chiesa, Lorenzo 2011, Notes towards a Manifesto for Metacritical Realism. http://www.diaphanes.de/titel/notes-towards-a-manifesto-for-metacritical-realism-1267. Accessed: 23 November 2017.

Chiesa, Lorenzo and Frank Ruda 2011, 'The Event of Language as Form of Life: Agamben's Linguistic Vitalism', *Angelaki: Journal of the Theoretical Humanities*, 16: 2.

Chiesa, Lorenzo and Alberto Toscano (eds.) 2009, *The Italian Difference: Between Nihilism and Biopolitics,* Melbourne: Re.press.

Cohen, Esther 1986, 'Law, Folklore and Animal Lore', *Past & Present*, 110: 6–37.

Croce, Benedetto 1969, *What Is Living and What Is Dead of the Philosophy of Hegel*, trans. Douglas Ainslie, New York: Russell & Russel.

Deleuze, Gilles 1997, *Critical and Clinical*, trans. Daniel W. Smith and Michael A. Greco, Minneapolis: University of Minnesota Press.

Deleuze, Gilles 2010, *L'abécédaire de. A comme Animal*, trans. Dominique Hurth, Maastricht: Jan van Eyck Academy.

Deleuze, Gilles and Felix Guattari 1986, *Kafka: Toward a Minor Literature*, trans. Dana Polan, Minneapolis: University of Minnesota Press.

Deleuze, Gilles and Felix Guattari 2005, *A Thousand Plateaus: Capitalism and Schizophrenia*, trans. Brian Massumi, Minneapolis: University of Minnesota Press.

Derrida, Jacques 1969, 'The Ends of Man', trans. Edouard Morot-Sir, Wesley C. Puisol, Hubert L. Dreyfus and Barbara Reid, *Philosophy and Phenomenological Research*, 30(1): 31–57.

Derrida, Jacques 1978, *Writing and Difference*, trans. Alan Bass, Chicago: The University of Chicago Press.

Derrida, Jacques 1990, *Heidegger et la question: De l'esprit et autres essais*, Paris: Flammarion.

Derrida, Jacques 2003, '*And Say the Animal Responded?*' trans. Daniel W. Smith and Michael A. Greco, *Zoontologies: The Question of the Animal*, Minneapolis: University of Minnesota Press.

Derrida, Jacques 2006, *L'animal que donc je suis*, Paris: Galilée.

Derrida, Jacques 2008, *The Animal That Therefore I Am*, trans. David Wills, New York: Fordham University Press.

Derrida, Jacques 2009–2011, *The Beast and the Sovereign*, Volumes 1 & 2, trans. Geoffrey Bennington, ed. Lisse, Michel, Marie-Louise Mallet and Ginette Michaud, Chicago: University of Chicago Press.

Descartes, Rene 1985, *The Philosophical Writings of Descartes*, Volume 1–2, trans. John Cottingham, Robert Stoothoff, Dugald Murdoch, Cambridge: Cambridge University Press.

Dolar, Mladen 2006, *A Voice and Nothing More*, Cambridge, MA: The MIT Press.

Dolar, Mladen 2008, 'Telephone and Psychoanalysis', Ljubljana: *Filozofski Vestnik* (in Slovene), 1: 7–24.

Dolar, Mladen 2012, 'Hegel and Freud', *e-flux*, 34 (4): http://www.e-flux.com/journal/34/68360/hegel-and-freud/. Accessed: 17 October 2017.

Evans, Edward Payson 1906, *The Criminal Prosecution and Capital Punishment of Animals*, New York: Dutton.

Fitzpatrick, Sheila 2004, 'Happiness and Toska: An Essay on the History of Emotions in Pre-War Soviet Russia', *Australian Journal of Politics and History*, 50(3): 357–371.

Flatley, Jonathan 2008, *Affective Mapping: Melancholia and the Politics of Modernism*, London: Harvard University Press.

Fontenay, Elisabeth de 1998, *Le silence des bêtes. La philosophie à l'épreuve de l'animalité*, Paris: Fayard.

Foucault, Michel 1965, *Madness and Civilization. A History of Insanity in the Age of Reason*, New York: Pantheon Books.

Foucault, Michel 1973, *The Order of Things: An Archaeology of the Human Sciences*, trans. Alan Sheridan, New York: Vintage Random House.

Foucault, Michel 2006, *History of Madness*, trans. Jonathan Murphy and Jean Khalfa, London: Routledge.

Girgen, Jen 2003, 'The Historical and Contemporary Prosecution and Punishment of Animals', *Animal Law Review at Lewis & Clark Law School*, 9: 97–133.

Günther, Hans 2012, 'A Mixture of Living Creatures: Man and Animal in the Works of Andrei Platonov', *Ulbandus: The Slavic Review of Columbia University*, 14: 251–272.

Hardt, Michael and Antonio Negri 2000, *Empire*, Cambridge, MA; London, England: Harvard University Press.

Harold, Bloom (ed.) 2003, *Franz Kafka*, New York: Chelsea House Publishers.

Hegel, G.W.F. 1931, *Jenenser Realphilosophie II, Die Vorlesungen von 1805–6*. Leipzig: Meiner.

Hegel, G.W.F. 1932, *Jenenser Realphilosophie I, Die Vorlesungen von 1803–4*, Leipzig: Meiner.

Hegel, G.W.F. 1967, *Philosophy of Right*, trans. T.M. Knox, Oxford: Oxford University Press.

Hegel, G.W.F. 1969, *Science of Logic*, trans. A.V. Miller, London: George Allen & Unwin Ltd.

Hegel, G.W.F. 1979, *Phenomenology of Spirit*, trans. A.V. Miller, Oxford: Oxford University Press.

Hegel, G.W.F. 1998, *Aesthetics. Lectures on Fine Art*, trans. T.M. Knox, Oxford: Oxford University Press.

Hegel, G.W.F. 2007, *Philosophy of Nature. Part Two of the Encyclopaedia of the Philosophical Sciences*, trans. A.V. Miller, Oxford: Oxford University Press.

Heidegger, Martin 1992, *Parmenides*, trans. Andre Schuwer and Richard Rojcewicz, Bloomington: Indiana University Press.

Heidegger, Martin 1995, *The Fundamental Concepts of Metaphysics: World, Finitude, Solitude*, trans. William McNeill and Nicholas Walker, Bloomington: Indiana University Press.

Heidegger, Martin 1998, 'Letter on Humanism', trans. Frank A. Capuzzi, *Pathmarks*, ed. Will MacNeill, Cambridge: Cambridge University Press.

Hyde, Walter 1916, 'The Prosecution and Punishment of Animals and Lifeless Things in the Middle Ages and Modern Times', *University of Pennsylvania Law Review*, 64: 696–730.

Hyppolite, Jean 1969, *Studies on Marx and Hegel*, trans. John O'neill, New York: Harper & Row Publishers.

Jameson, Fredric 1994, *The Seeds of Time*, New York: Columbia University Press.

Jameson, Fredric 2010, *The Hegel Variations: On the Phenomenology of Spirit*, New York: Verso.

Kafka, Franz 1995, *The Complete Stories*, trans. Willa and Edwin Muir, New York: Schocken Books.

Khlebnikov, Velimir 2008, Председатель земного шара: Стихотворения, поэмы, статьи, декларации, заметки [*President of the Globe: Poems, Articles, Declarations, Notes*], Saint Petersburg: Azbuka-Classica.

Kilpatrick, David 2008, 'Sacrificial Simulacra from Nietzsche to Nitsch', *Hyperion*, 3: 3.

Kojève, Alexander 1969, *Introduction to the Reading of Hegel*, trans. James H. Nichols, Jr., Ithaca: Cornell University Press.

Lacan, Jacques 1977, *Ecrits, A Selection*, trans. Alan Sheridan, New York: W.W. Norton & Co.

Lacan, Jacques 1991a, *The Seminar of Jacques Lacan, Book 1: Freud's Papers on Technique 1953–4*, trans. John Forrester, London: W.W. Norton & Company.

Lacan, Jacques 1991b, *The Seminar of Jacques Lacan, Book II: The Ego in Freud's Theory and in the Technique of Psychoanalysis, 1954–1955*, trans. Sylvana Tomaselli, New York; London: W.W. Norton & Company.

Lacan, Jacques 1998, *The Seminar of Jacques Lacan, Book XI: The Four Fundamental Concepts of Psychoanalysis*, trans. Alan Sheridan, New York; London: W.W. Norton & Company.

Lane, Tora 2012, 'A Groundless Foundation Pit', *Ulbandus: The Slavic Review of Columbia University*, 14: 61–75.

Lawrence, D.H. 1995, *Birds, Beasts and Flowers*, Santa Rosa: Black Sparrow Press.

Leibniz, Gottfried 1890, *The Philosophical Works of Leibniz*, trans. George Martin Duncan, New Haven: Yale University Press.

Levinas, Emmanuel 1979, *Totality and Infinity: An Essay on Exteriority*, trans. Alphonso Lingis, The Hague; Boston; London: Martinus Nijhoff Publishers.

Lindberg, Susanna 2004, 'Heidegger's Animal', In *Phenomenological Studies*, Hrsg. von Ernst Wolfgang Orth und Karl-Heinz Lembeck, Hamburg: Felix Meiner Verlag.

Lippit, Akira Mizuta 2000, *Electric/Animal: Toward a Rhetoric of Wildlife*, Minneapolis; London: University of Minnesota Press.

Malabou, Catherine 1996, 'Who's Afraid of Hegelian Wolves?' *Deleuze: A Critical Reader*, ed. Paul Patton, Oxford: Blackwell Publishers.

Malabou, Catherine 2005, *The Future of Hegel: Plasticity, Temporality and Dialectics*, trans. Lisabeth During, London; New York: Routledge.

Marx, Karl and Frederick Engels 1976, *Collected Works*. Volume 5. 1845–7, trans. C. Dutt, W. Lough and C.P. Magill, New York: International Publishers.

Marx, Karl and Frederick Engels 2009, *Economic and Philosophic Manuscripts of 1844*, trans. Martin Milligan, Marxist.org, https://www.marxists.org/archive/marx/works/download/pdf/Economic-Philosophic-Manuscripts-1844.pdf. Accessed: 17 October 2017.

Maurizi, Marco 2012, 'The Dialectical Animal: Nature and Philosophy of History in Adorno, Horkheimer and Marcuse', *Journal for Critical Animal Studies*, 10(1): 67–103.

Nancy, Jean-Luc 1991a, *The Inoperative Community*, ed. and trans. Peter Connor, Lisa Garbus, Michael Holland and Simona Sawhney., Minneapolis: University of Minnesota Press.

Nancy, Jean-Luc 1991b, 'The Unsacrificiable', *Yale French Studies*, No. 79, Literature and the Ethical Question: 20–38.

Nancy, Jean-Luc 2002, *Hegel: The Restlessness of the Negative*, trans. Jason Smith and Steven Miller, Minneapolis; London: University of Minnesota Press.

Nancy, Jean-Luc 2004, *La communauté désœuvrée*, Paris: Christian Bourgois Éditeur.

Noys, Benjamin 2000, *Georges Bataille: A Critical Introduction*, London: Pluto Press.

Noys, Benjamin 2010, *The Persistence of the Negative: A Critique of Contemporary Continental Theory*, Edinburgh: Edinburgh University Press.

Noys, Benjamin 2011, 'The Poverty of Vitalism (and the Vitalism of Poverty)', *To Have Done with Life: Vitalism and Anti-vitalism in Contemporary Philosophy* (Zagreb, conference paper).

Plato 1934, *The Laws, Book IX*, trans. A.E. Taylor, London: J.M. Dent & Sons Ltd.

Platonov, Andrei 1978, *Chevengur*, trans. Anthony Olcott, Michigan: Ann Arbor Press.

Platonov, Andrei 1984, *Собрание сочинений* [*Selected Works*], Volume 3, Moscow: Soviet Russia.

Platonov, Andrei 1989, *Живя главной жизнью* [*Living the Main Life*], Moscow: Pravda.

Platonov, Andrei 1990a, *На заре туманной юности: Повести и рассказы* [*On the Sunset of a Hazy Youth, Novels and Stories*], Moscow: Soviet Russia.

Platonov, Andrei 1999, *The Return and Other Stories*, trans. Robert Chandler, Elizabeth Chandler and Angela Livingstone, London: Harvill Press.

Platonov, Andrei 2005, 'Der Antisexus', *Am Nullpunkt. Am Nullpunkt. Positionen der russischen Avantgarde.* Hrsg. von Boris Groys und Aage Hansen-Löve. Frankfurt: Suhrkamp Verlag, 494–505.

Platonov, Andrei 2008, *Soul and Other Stories*, trans. Robert Chandler and Elizabeth Chandler, New York: NURB.

Platonov, Andrei 2009, *The Foundation Pit*, New York: NYRB.

Platonov, Andrei 2011, *On the First Socialist Tragedy*, trans. Tony Wood, *New Left Review*, 69: 312.

Platonov, Andrey 2013, *The Anti-Sexus*, trans. Anne .O. Fisher, *Cabinet* 51: 48–53.

Podoroga, Valery 1991, 'Eunuch of the Soul: Positions of Reading and the World of Platonov', *Perestroyka: Perspectives on Modernisation, The South Atlantic Quarterly*, 90(2) 355–356.

Podoroga, Valery 2011, *Мимесис: Материалы по аналитической анропологии литературы* [*Mimesis: Materials on Analytical Anthropology of Literature*], Volume 1–2, Moscow: Cultural Revolution.

Pushkin, Alexander 1991, *Eugene Onegin*, trans. Vladimir Nabokov, Princeton: Princeton University Press.

Rand, Sebastian 2010, 'Animal Subjectivity and the Nervous System in Hegel's Philosophy of Nature', *Revista Eletrônica Estudos Hegelianos*. Published in Portuguese as "Subjetividade animal e o sistema nervoso na Filosofia da Natureza de Hegel," Revista Eletrônica Estudos Hegelianos, 7:12 [2010].

Rohman, Carrie 2009, *Stalking the Subject: Modernism and the Animal*. New York, Columbia University Press.

Simondon, Gilbert 1964, *L'Individu et sa genèse physico-biologique*. Paris: PUF.

Simondon, Gilbert 2009, 'The Position of the Problem of Ontogenesis', trans. Gregory Flanders, *Parrhesia*, 7: 4–16.

Simondon, Gilbert 2011, *Two Lessons on Animal and Man*, trans. Drew S. Burk. Minneapolis: Univocal Publishing.

Sofronov, Vladislav 2009, *Коммунизм чувственности: Читая Кьеркегора, Пруста, Кафку, Маркса* [*Communism of Sensitivity: Reading Kierkegaard, Proust, Kafka, and Marx*], Moscow: Territory of the Future.

Timofeeva, Oxana 2009, *Введение в эротическую философию Жоржа Батая* [*Introduction to the Erotic Philosophy of Georges Bataille*], Moscow: New Literary Observer.

Timofeeva, Oxana 2011, 'Бедная жизнь: Зоотехник Високовский против философа Хайдеггера' ['Poor Life: Animal Technician Visokovsky Against Philosopher Heidegger'], *New Literary Observer*, 106: 96–113.

Timofeeva, Oxana 2013, 'The Negative Animal', *Stasis*, 1: 266–289.

Timofeeva, Oxana 2014, 'The End of the World: From Apocalypse to the End of History And Back', *e-flux*, 56(6), http://www.e-flux.com/journal/the-end-of-the-world-from-apocalypse-to-the-end-of-history-and-back/. Accessed: 17 October 2017.

Timofeeva, Oxana 2015a, 'Unconscious Desire for Communism', *Identities: Journal for Politics, Gender, and Culture*, 11: 32–48.

Timofeeva, Oxana 2015b, 'Uninvited Animals', In *Valley of Beggars*, Eds. Katerina Chuchalina, Vladislav Shapovalov. Venice: Marsilio editori, 59–82.

Waldau, P. and K. Patton (eds.) 2006, *A Communion of Subjects: Animals in Religion, Science and Ethics*, New York: Columbia University Press.

Wolfe, Cary (ed.) 2003, *Zoontologies: The Question of the Animal*, Minneapolis: University of Minnesota Press.

Wood, David 1999, '*Comment ne pas manger* – Deconstruction and Humanism', *Animal Others: On Ethics, Ontology and Animal Life*, ed. H. Peter Steeves, Albany: State University of New York Press, 15–36.

Zabolotsky, Nikolay 2005, 'Selections from the Triumph of Agriculture',
    trans. Eugene Ostashevsky, *http://www.thefreelibrary.com/
    Selections+from+The+Triumph+of+Agriculture.-a0134043717*.
    Accessed: 17 October 2017.
Žižek, Slavoj (ed.) 1998, *Cogito and the Unconscious*, Durham: Duke
    University Press.
Žižek, Slavoj 2010, *Living in the End Times*, London: Verso.
Žižek, Slavoj 2012, *Less than Nothing: Hegel and the Shadow of Dialectical
    Materialism*, London: Verso.

Index